RYAN HUNT

Self-Confidence

First edition

This book was professionally typeset on Reedsy.
Find out more at reedsy.com

Contents

Introduction

One of the most important elements of success is self-confidence. A lot of studies and research have been done to fully understand the concept of believing in oneself and how it can lead to a successful life. There are many successful individuals in your personal life that you can look up to. It can be your parents who have raised you and your siblings to be good people who have stable careers.

It can be a friend who has overcome alcoholism and has been sober for several years now. Or it can be an acquaintance who runs her own business and travels the world in her free time. Even when you do not know someone personally, you can just look around you and you will see a lot of successful individuals—be it a celebrity, a businessman, athlete, an artist, a career person, etc.

Aside from these amazing individuals, two groups of people stand out when it comes to being successful in everything that they do—the ancient Spartans and the Special Operations Forces. They may have come from two very different periods but the principles that they adhere to are more or less the same, which makes them highly successful groups of people.

What makes the Spartans and Special Forces so unique? They are confident in everything that they do, otherwise, they will not be able to complete their training but you cannot simply lump them together with famous successful individuals such as Elon Musk or Peter Thiel. Their training is different because it encompasses physical, mental, emotional, and even spiritual toughness. The successful individuals that you see all around you are admirable, but what sets the Spartans and the Special Operations Forces apart from these groups of people is self-confidence which stems from courage. Self-confidence is one thing, but having courage is a whole different level. You will learn more about how courage and fearlessness make a person more confident in everything that he does that leads to success when you start reading this book. You can apply the timeless principles used by the Spartans and Special Operations Forces to gain admiration and respect from your peers.

In this book, you will learn many different things about self-confidence and fearlessness in relation to the training of the Spartans and Special Operations Forces.

Some important points will be discussed in this book, such as:

- Reasons why some people do not have self-confidence while others do not have a hard time believing in themselves
- Ways on improving physical, emotional, and mental health
- Techniques on how to take action and not just become a passive observer of the lives of successful people
- Useful tips to overcome adversities in your life
- Ways to get rid of fear to achieve self-confidence
- Tips on how to stop doing bad habits and start doing good ones
- Ways to become efficient, effective, and confident even on your worst days
- Methods of defining your goals and objectives and how to achieve them the best way possible
- Ideas on how to focus on your positive traits and assets and revealing talents that you do not know you have
- Important behavior to have to achieve self-love and positive self-view
- How to live a life free from fears and worries

These are just some of the things that you will learn as you start reading this book. Start your journey to a more confident life right now!

1

The Spartans and the Special Operations Forces

Who are the Spartans?

The first thing that you need to do is to learn more about the Spartans. You have most likely heard of them from books, movies, and pop culture. The Spartans are known for their self-discipline and fearlessness. They lived in Sparta, a Greek town situated in the southern Peloponnesian region. Today, Sparta is just like any other modern urban jungle, with concrete blocks of apartments and offices. Thousands of years ago, just hearing the name Sparta sparked fear, admiration, and reverence because the place was home to the most powerful warriors in ancient Greece, the Spartans. Countless stories have been written about them because their training is something to be admired. They became successful warriors and beat even the most powerful of rivals because of the kind of discipline they had.

Aside from self-discipline and fearlessness, the Spartans are also known for their humble society. Ancient Greece back then, especially in major places like Athens, favored creating sophisticated structures made of marble. Sparta, on the other hand, maintained its cultural values of simplicity and austerity, with most of its structures built from wood and other simple yet sturdy materials. They focused mostly on military training and did not bother with frivolous and luxurious things. Their life revolved around being a successful warrior society—from the time a Spartan baby was born up to his death. This is probably one of the things that made them extremely successful warriors—their goal was clear and straightforward and every little thing that they did was geared towards achieving this goal.

Their education system called the agoge was all about training the little boys to become exceptional soldiers. It is like a boot camp from daycare to college. They were also taught basic arithmetic, reading, and writing because a great warrior must also have basic knowledge of things but the education system was mostly about building physical and mental toughness by undergoing intensive training and dangerous exercises.

In today's world, the kind of training that the Spartans had to go through may not be applicable but you can learn a lot of things from these extraordinary people.

How did the Spartans train?

Human rights are not a common topic back in the day and you will see a lot of violations in how the Spartans trained. However, you can still learn a lot from these ancient warriors in terms of the kind of mindset that you should have to be self-confident. So what kind of training did the Spartans undergo?

· Training started from infancy

When a Spartan baby was born, he had to be inspected by a council to see if the baby was fit to become a soldier in the future. If physical defects were observed, the baby would be left to die or thrown at the foot of the mountain, although the latter was considered a myth by most historians. If the child was lucky, he would be rescued by strangers. If not, he would either die from animal attacks, exposure to the elements, or hunger and thirst.

The lives of those babies who were considered fit to become soldiers in the future were not a walk in the park, either. When they started crying, the mothers would not pick them up. They would just leave them until they stop. The babies were also left in the dark by themselves to train to be fearless and were bathed in wine instead of plain water. This was considered 'tough love' and it was so popular in ancient Greece even in neighboring states that Spartan women were highly regarded as excellent mothers and nurses.

· The Agoge education system

The state-sponsored education system in Sparta, called the Agoge, started when the boys turned 7. They had to be separated from their families to begin the difficult training regimen. Although the Agoge system was designed to train them to become exceptional soldiers and exemplary citizens when they

4

grow up, the boys were still taught academics, the arts, and other subjects that are more or less military-related such as hunting, stealth, warfare, and sports. Older students aged 12 were forced to sleep outside with nothing to wear but a red cloak. Stealing food from others or scavenging was encouraged but anyone who got caught would be punished, usually by flogging. These exercises taught them how to be resilient against the elements, resourceful despite having limited materials on hand, and stealthy especially when they had to cross over enemy lines.

· Physical punishments and brawls

In modern days, hazing is still being practiced by certain organizations such as fraternities; it is not encouraged. In Sparta, hazing and fighting were encouraged to build tough men out of the Spartan boys. Adults and teachers would encourage fighting among younger boys and physical punishment was practiced because it made the boys tougher and entirely removed any form of timidity or cowardice. Physical punishments made it easier for them to endure hardships such as pain and hunger. Teasing and ridicule that often led to brawls also made the boys mentally stronger.

There was even a religious ritual that involved flogging of the Spartan boys that sometimes led to death called the "diamastigosis". This was done at the sanctuary Artemis Orthia in front of an altar. This also served as a physical test for courage and pain endurance. As time went by and Sparta was no longer considered a military powerhouse, this practice became a blood sport done in amphitheaters where spectators watched and cheered.

· The Spartan diet

At age 21, a student of the agoge would be allowed to eat at a military-style mess called the "syssitia". This was where citizens ate their meals. You might think that there was a buffet and the food was a feast but this was far from what they served at the syssitia. The main purpose of the mess was to prepare soldiers for war when food was scarce, which is why they served bland, unflavored, and insufficient meals. They also discouraged being overweight and unfit, so overeating was highly discouraged. The Spartans were well known for their strict diet and exercise regiment which made them physically fit. People who were overweight were loathed and ridiculed and were also at risk of being permanently banished from Sparta. When it comes to drinking, Spartans loved drinking wine but drunkenness was frowned upon. In fact, they would make Helots drunk and allowed them to act wildly, which they would then show to their children as an example of why getting drunk was not a good thing.

· The Spartan women

While boys were trained to become skilled warriors, the Spartan girls were trained to become mothers and wives of Spartan soldiers. They did not have to leave their homes and stayed with their parents but their education and training system were just as intensive and rigorous. Spartan women should bear children and should train to become strong and tough mothers. Their subjects include physical activities such as discus throwing, javelin, gymnastics, and dancing. The girls would ridicule and shame trainees who were lagging while performing a song in front of the Spartan dignitaries.

· The different classes in the Spartan society

Since the society was all about the military and producing elite soldiers, it is not surprising that the highest class in Sparta was the military class called the "Homoioi". If a man wanted to become an equal citizen, the only option was to become a soldier. Being in the military was not only a career but it was also a way of life and it dictated a man's place in society. It was a lifelong commitment because a soldier could remain on duty until they reached 60.

You might ask, how could this type of society survive if the only thing that mattered for them was the military? They also had trades and manufacturing but the people who worked in these areas were considered inferior as compared to the military men. People who were not in the military and instead worked as laborers, craftsmen, and traders belonged to the lower class in the Spartan society called the "Perioeci". They were free but were considered as non-citizens and they lived in Laconia.

Meanwhile, the "Helots" or the slaves who worked in agriculture and were generally responsible for the food production were the lowest class. It is interesting to note that the Spartans focused so much on building a strong military because there was always a threat of the Helots, which comprised the majority of the Spartan population, revolting against the state.

· Marriage was encouraged

The Spartans were not discouraged to have relationships and get married but the main reason for getting married was to conceive more Spartan soldiers. Because of this, citizens of the state were encouraged to choose partners who were physically fit and healthy so that they would produce babies who had a higher chance of becoming excellent soldiers. Men were supposed to stay inside the military barracks until they reached the age of 30, which means that they would be separated from their wives if they married young. Marriage, giving birth, and child-rearing were strictly monitored by the Spartan government. If a male Spartan could not make his wife pregnant, he had to allow his wife to be impregnated by a virile male so that they would have children. Male Spartans who were at the right age to get married but had not yet tied the knot would be subject to mockery and ridicule because it was seen as shirking from their responsibilities.

· Surrendering was not an option

Surrendering to their enemies was considered cowardice. It was seen as a disgrace, and soldiers who surrendered despite putting up a good fight were shamed by their peers that most of them just ended up killing themselves. Spartan soldiers were expected to fight to the death. It was either winning or die fighting. Soldiers who surrendered could only redeem themselves by later on dying in battle, if they did not commit suicide first.

If you think their wives or mothers would take their husbands' or sons' sides, you are wrong because Spartan women also had a do-or-die approach when it came to wars or battles. It was said that they would tell the line "return with your shield or on it" to their husbands or sons when sending them to war, which means that they should only come back home as a successful combatant or a dead soldier who dies fighting. Both of these scenarios were considered as soldiers fulfilling their duties to the state. In Sparta, only soldiers who died fighting in war and women who died in childbirth were the only ones who could have their names on their tombstones.

Who Are The Special Operations Forces?

The Special Operations Forces are probably the closest counterpart of the Spartans in these modern times. These are military units that conduct special operations such as anti-terrorism activities, sabotage, hostage rescue, counter-insurgency, unconventional warfare, and scouting or reconnaissance. These operations require speed, stealth, special tactics, and quick thinking which is why people who belong to the Special Operations Forces require intensive training of the body and mind.

Some of the most famous Special Operations Forces in the United States are the Navy SEALS, Force RECON, Marine Raiders, Green Berets, Rangers, Night Stalkers, and Air Force Special Tactics, to name a few. These are groups inside the Army, Navy,Marines and Air Force but they undergo more advanced and rigorous to be able to perform Special Operations tasks. Other countries also have their elite forces such as SAS or the British Special Air Service, the Special Boat Service which is the Navy SEAL counterpart in the U.K., SayeretMatkal in Israel, National Gendarmerie Intervention Group in France, the Russian Alpha Group, and the Unidad de OperacionesEspeciales in Spain.

How do the Special Operations Forces train?

The training of these groups of soldiers is different from the training of the Spartans but the principle is more or less the same—developing stamina, fearlessness, and mental strength to be able to succeed in military activities.

· Physical training

1. One of the most important skills to master as a Special Operations soldier is running. You should run at least 25 to 30 miles per week if you want to avoid injuries such as knee tendonitis or shin splints. You will not only be running fast but you will be running with a heavy load on your back. Your lungs and legs must be always prepared to run.
2. A Special Operations soldier will be carrying heavy loads on his back such as backpacks with all his supplies, logs, or even an injured comrade. It is

important to maintain a strong lower back. There are special exercises to strengthen the lower back such as body drags, dead lift, fireman carries, farmer walks, and hang clean. If you are not carrying a heavy load on your back while walking, you will be standing all day, which also puts a strain on the back.

3. You might be required to swim in a body of water as part of the Special Operations that you have to participate in. Normal swimming activity is a great aerobic exercise but you should also practice survival swimming, wherein you have to swim in the water with your full military uniform and combat boots on. While in battle or doing some other Special Operations tasks, you will not have the luxury to change to proper swimming attire. You have to swim in the water with your clothes and boots on. You might want to improve your swimming skills first by doing regular lapses in the pool before training for survival swimming.

These are just some examples of physical training that an elite soldier has to undergo. There are many more types of exercises that focus on different parts of the body and are more difficult to execute but these are better left explained at the boot camp, if you ever decide to become a Special Operations soldier.

· Land navigation

Being able to read the map and the compass is a must if you want to pass the Special Operations training with flying colors. You will not always be assigned to a familiar location. More often than not, Special Operations soldiers are sent overseas or to an unfamiliar territory, and they must know how to go to their intended destination or to lead their troops back to their camp.

· Combatives

The Elite Forces also have to train different forms of hand-to-hand combat such as Jiujitsu. This teaches soldiers how to fight without using advanced weapons and at the same time the training instills in them the values of a great warrior and the confidence of knowing that their own body is enough to win a fight against the enemy.

· Sniper training

This is not just about hitting your target from afar. Sniper training also involves surveillance and the use of ballistic computers. Digital photography is also taught because some situations require taking photos of subjects or areas. This may sound morbid but they are also taught the proper use of a semi-automatic rifle to hollow out the skull of the target. The main purpose of learning how to shoot is to ensure that you do it properly. If the command is to shoot to kill, then the enemy has to be killed in one shot.

There is another form of sniper shooting called aerial platform support where the sniper has to shoot the target while in a moving helicopter. This is a more advanced sniper skill because the shooter is moving and the target can be either stationary or in motion.

· Explosive breaching

This is when they have to enter an enemy structure or compound by destroying an entrance. You have probably seen this done in movies where the soldiers blow down a metal door or other blockages to enter an enemy building. Doing this is not only a quick and efficient way to gain entry but it also adds an element of shock and surprise to the bad guys. This is a lot more than bombing a door because it requires technical skill when it comes to deciding the kind of explosive to use. Moreover, they are not allowed to fail the first attempt because it gives the enemy a warning that someone is trying to break in.

· Helocasting and fast-roping

This is another infiltration technique that the elite forces have to train for before they go to their mission. This is when the helicopter flies low over a body of water and the soldier is expected to jump and swim to shore where the enemies are. This is of course done when the place being infiltrated is surrounded by a body of water. These days, this is not commonly being used because most of the operations and missions are done in the desert or mountains.

Another similar technique is fast-roping where the soldiers have to slide down or climb up a braided rope attached to a moving helicopter for insertion or extraction purposes. This can be tricky because soldiers usually carry heavy combat equipment which is why proper training is necessary.

· Mobility

Soldiers have to drive different kinds of special operation vehicles such as armored gun trucks, ATVs, and dirt bikes. The last two are highly utilized in Afghanistan because of the kind of terrain in the area. Another type of vehicle is a tactical vehicle that looks normal from the outside but carries combat equipment such as rocket launchers, hand grenades, and bullets. Special Operations soldiers are also taught how to shoot while driving at the same time.

· Combat diving

Maritime special operations require proper training which includes aquatic and subsurface infiltration. Special scuba diving equipment and re-breathers are used so that the soldiers underwater will not produce bubbles or other indications that someone is underwater just waiting to resurface. The kind of training that they have to go through is now only about diving but also about drown-proofing, physics, navigation underwater, physiology, operation of small boats, use of kayak and inflatable boats, and many more.

- Military free-fall

You have seen in the movies how elite soldiers jump off an airplane with their parachutes on. This is a real-life skill that special operations soldiers have to learn. There are two types of parachuting—high-altitude high-opening and high-altitude low-opening. The high altitude makes it difficult for the jumpers to breathe that is why they have to be on oxygen during the process. The difference between the two is the distance of the soldier from the ground before deploying the parachute. The first type is when the parachute is deployed at 30,000 feet above ground or immediately after jumping off the plane while the second type is when the parachute is deployed at only 4,000 feet above ground. This is difficult because the soldiers have to wear the full combat uniform and are expected to fight almost as soon as they touch the ground.

- Rapport-building

So what is rapport-building exactly? Are the Special Operations Forces expected to be friends with their enemies? This is about building a strong relationship with an ally—this could be a host country or a counterpart unit whom you have to work with side by side. It is important that you get along with these people and you have trust and good communication if you want your special operation mission to succeed. You might have excellent combat skills, technical know-how, and advanced military equipment but knowing how to handle people, especially potential allies is equally, if not more important.

These are the things that the Spartans and Special Operations Forces have to go through to complete their training. The difficulty of these training exercises and completing them are a huge factor in the self-confidence of these warriors and soldiers.

This does not mean, however, that you need to undergo the same training. What is important is that you focus on the things that make the Spartans and Special Operations Forces confident in what they do. And the major common factor is courage or fearlessness.

But first, you have to understand the psychology of confidence by reading the next few chapters.

2

What is confidence?

You have probably read and heard about self-confidence throughout your life ever since you can remember. How many times have you heard your parents tell you to be more confident when in school, or to be more confident when answering questions during an interview? What is confidence, exactly?

This may sound cheesy, but confidence is believing in yourself, your skills, and your abilities. It is having positive regard for and views towards yourself. The word 'confidence' itself has its roots from the Latin 'fidere' which means 'trust'. Therefore, having self-confidence is trusting yourself.

How to know if you have confidence? You know that you can handle anything that life throws at you. You are more in tune and relaxed with your life and your response to everything seems smooth and natural. For you, and maybe those people around you, everything looks easy or everything has a solution. This is because you believe in your abilities and what you can do. Keep in mind that this is different from being arrogant because arrogance is shouting to the whole world that you are the best. Confidence is quiet and the result of your actions speaks for itself. Arrogance makes people dislike you. Confidence, on the other hand, inspires.

Just look at the Spartans and Special Operations Forces. The Spartans have long been gone as a society but their principles still live on. They left a mark in history as some of the most fearless and confident people that have ever graced this planet. The Special Operations Forces are also known for their excellence in everything they do and their confidence in the way they handle sensitive operations. This is what you should strive to be.

Confidence is also reflected in how others see you because it is apparent in how you look and sound. Just keep in mind though that having self-confidence is not enough to be charismatic and an inspiration to others and have. It also depends on your communication skills and how you build rapport with the people you talk to.

Self-esteem and self-confidence

These are two words that have been used interchangeably. You already know that self-confidence is your belief in your capabilities. Self-esteem, on the other hand, is your sense of self or your self-worth. Although it may seem logical that people who have high self-confidence would have high self-esteem, this is not always the case. Just look at the number of successful and confident artists who could perform in front of thousands of people but later on killed themselves. They are confident in their craft, but they have a poor sense of self-worth. It can also be the other way around. You may have high self-esteem and you know that you are worthy but yet you do not have the confidence to do certain things, such as talking in public or acing that exam.

People with high self-esteem are those who do not care about having a high income, status, or other materialistic pursuits because they believe these things do not define their value as a person. They do not need to rely on crutches such as drugs or alcohol.

This is a higher form of cognitive principle that you should also aim for. But this can be easier to achieve if you first take care of your self-confidence issues. When you start believing in your capabilities as an individual, then nurturing your self-worth will be much easier to tackle.

Self-confidence—nature vs nurture?

In psychology, the question nature vs nurture always appears in almost all kinds of discussion, including topics about self-confidence. Why are some people more confident than others? Why does confidence come more easily to some people while others have a difficult time with it? Are some people naturally gifted with confidence, while others have to suffer from the lack of it? Can it be learned?

Like most subjects in psychology, self-confidence is partially a natural occurrence in our genes, which means that some people are genetically wired to be confident. You will see this among children. Some children naturally radiate confidence, while others need gentle probing. Other factors may play in this as well such as shyness. This does not mean, however, that confidence cannot be developed later on in life. You probably have a coworker who always seems unfazed by criticisms. His feathers do not get ruffled. Or you probably have a friend who is not afraid to try new things or take risks. They are also not sure whether they would succeed or not, but they go for it anyway. Why? What do they have that you do not?

These people may have always had confidence in themselves from the time they could do things on their own, but it is also possible that they developed their confidence as they grow older.

That is the beauty of it all. You can teach yourself to become more self-confident. The proof is in the way the Spartans trained all their children who were born healthy to become great warriors. For sure not all of them were born with innate confidence. But they were trained to be fearless and become confident. This is the same thing with the Special Operations soldiers. These men most likely came from different backgrounds, childhood, and upbringing. When they started the training, they did not have the confidence to use a grenade or jump off a plane, or shoot to kill. But after their training, they became more confident in their ability to do these things and also in general.

You can also undergo a kind of training to make yourself more confident. So to answer the question why are some people more confident than others, the genetic makeup of an individual partly contributes to that, but the nurturing part is the bigger factor. Just learn about the different kinds of training that you need to do to be more confident in yourself.

The good thing about training yourself to be fearless and confident is that the more you move towards it, the more your potential expands. It means that you will continuously learn things about yourself and your capabilities as you pursue your goal to become more confident.

To illustrate, on your journey to becoming more confident in your work as a regular employee, you might realize that you have the potential to become a manager because you are good with people and handling issues in your workplace. This is because you are starting to try new things. And the more you try new things, the more you learn about yourself and reveal abilities that you did not know you have.

You also need to know if you do not have confidence in yourself. It might not be clear to you that's why you should know how to tell so that you can address it properly and immediately. If you always doubt yourself and you think you cannot do a certain task, then you do not have self-confidence. For example, if your boss asks you to do a task for the first time, you find yourself worrying about it or worse, telling your boss that you cannot do it because you think you do not have the right skills. Or maybe you do not volunteer yourself to work on certain projects because you think you cannot do it as well as your coworker.

Another sign is when you receive negative feedback or criticism, it will eat up whatever confidence you have left and you will wallow in self-pity thinking you are not good enough. You focus too much on your mistakes, which makes it difficult for you to take on new projects because you still have that fear of receiving criticisms and negative feedback.

You also tend to ignore compliments and positive feedback. You just cannot believe that people would find your work great. You even have this gnawing fear of people finding out that you are just faking it. That you are not capable but you just got lucky.

These are also signs of having Imposter syndrome, which will be discussed more in-depth next.

Impostor syndrome

You might think it is just a simple case of not having confidence but you might have impostor syndrome. This phenomenon was first named by two psychologists, Suzanne Imes and Pauline Rose Clance in the late 1970s. And according to studies, this is not a one-of-a-kind occurrence because around 70% of people have experienced having feelings of being an impostor. This affects people from all walks of life but is more common among women and highly intelligent and successful people, according to some research.

Impostor syndrome is that feeling of being a fraud and that your successes in life are due to luck and not talent or hard work. You have this constant fear of being found out that you just faked your way towards your success. It is the feeling of not belonging. You think you are just part of the group because you got lucky.

So what are the signs of impostor syndrome?

- Doubting yourself
- Being too hard on yourself
- Thinking that your success is because of external factors like luck and not because of your ability and competence
- Undermining your skills and competence
- The constant fear of not living up to the expectation of others
- Sabotaging yourself because you would rather destroy your chances of success than failing
- Setting goals that are almost impossible and berating yourself when you

do not achieve it
· Being a perfectionist and an overachiever

Some might think that this is just a form of perfectionism but that is not the case because it is damaging to your success as an individual because of the anxiety that you always feel. You are over-preparing and working extra hard sp that nobody will find out that you are just faking it.

Imagine how it is like if you have impostor syndrome—something as simple as attending a family reunion will become a big deal. You will try to memorize details about your family members so that you will have something to talk about when you are left alone with them. Or you will stay up all night just to prepare for a small quiz because you are afraid of failing and of people finding out that you are not good enough.

What makes it even more difficult is that successfully doing something does not change the way you view yourself. For example, you might have aced that quiz or your aunts and uncles might have laughed at your jokes and thought you were the funniest relative but you would still see yourself the same way as before—a fraud. The more you become successful and the more accomplishments you have, the more you think of yourself as a fraud. It is like your brain cannot understand that you are good enough and that your successes are all because of you.

What triggers impostor syndrome? It may stem from a child's upbringing. Maybe you come from a family of overachievers and your parents are hard to please. Or maybe you are currently being offered a higher position with more responsibilities and you doubt yourself. Or maybe you are about to start attending a university when you are older and you feel like there are just too many young people and they will find out that you are ancient when you do not know how to use a computer. Things like these can cause impostor syndrome.

There are different variations of impostor syndrome and you must know about them so that you can get the right kind of help that you need.

- The perfectionist

Some might say that being a perfectionist is a good thing. But as they always say, too much of anything is not good. People who are perfectionists always set high goals for themselves, and when they cannot reach these goals, they berate themselves and start doubting their abilities. Aside from being too hard on themselves, perfectionists are not good team players because they would rather do things themselves instead of letting other people help. They tend to be micromanagers and control freaks. This is not a good trait of a leader because delegating tasks is difficult for them. Your work and everyone else's work should be 100% perfect at all times. This group does not experience satisfaction after reaching a goal because they always feel like they could have done more. They also tend to be slow starters and workers because they always wait for the perfect time to start and for everything to be in proper order before starting. They focus even on small, insignificant details, which makes them work slowly. One thing that perfectionists should remember is that successes should be celebrated to experience contentment and avoid the feeling of restlessness and burnout. This also greatly enhances self-confidence.

You need to tell yourself that mistakes are okay because they are part of the learning process. And it may sound like a cliché but you are only human and humans make mistakes. Even robots and machines make mistakes.

- The superwoman/superman

Since people with impostor syndrome think they are phonies, they often try to cover this up by working extra harder than the people around them. If you find yourself volunteering to work overtime even if you are done with your day's work because you feel like you have not done enough, then you probably belong to this group. You might also feel like you do not deserve your breaks even if you are finished with your work. You do not have hobbies or spend time just doing nothing because you feel like you should be doing more. Working harder and for longer hours somehow eases your insecurities and your self-doubts. It does not make sense because you have awards and degrees to back up your successes in life but you still think you are a phony among your colleagues. The superwomen and supermen find validation from working extra hard.

You might say that the Spartans and Special Operations Forces are all super-women and supermen in your opinion so why does this become a negative thing when translated to ordinary life? The Spartans and elite forces may have extraordinarily difficult goals but when they achieve these goals, such as coming out victorious in a war or completing a mission, they acknowledge whatever awards or compliments they get and they feel more confident in their abilities. This is something that you should learn from these great warriors and soldiers.

Moreover, you should stop focusing on external validation and focus instead on self-validation to start gaining more confidence. This way, you will cut yourself some slack and ease off the workload that you put upon yourself little by little.

• The natural genius

This group of people believes that they should be able to do things perfectly on their first attempt. They judge themselves based on how fast and easily they can successfully finish a project or understand a concept. They feel that if they take a long time to do something, albeit successfully, they feel ashamed because they think they do not have the talent or skill. What makes them different from perfectionists is that they do not only set impossibly high standards for themselves; they also want to successfully understand a concept or finish a project without spending too much time and effort on it. They feel like a fraud if they are having a more difficult time than usual to finish a task when this is just natural because no matter how smart you are, you will still find yourself struggling with other things.

If you are the type of person who always gets high grades and just navigates through tasks easily, and when you find yourself in a situation where you are struggling, you might feel ashamed of yourself. You also do not like working with a mentor or do not want others teaching you because you feel like you should learn things on your own without too much trouble. You might also avoid trying new things because you do not want to be uncomfortable and in a position where you do not know how to do things.

You should learn to accept the fact that you are a human being with flaws. You are not expected to know everything. Even the world's geniuses have weaknesses and have to make an effort to learn certain things. By letting go of your high expectations of yourself, you will be able to gain more confidence. You should also start opening up to the idea of learning things that are out of your comfort zone.

- The soloists

This is also related to the previous types of impostor syndromes because soloists also do not accept help from others, viewing it as a sign of incompetence. They believe that accomplishing things on their own is the only way to go. Being independent and being able to do things without the help of others is a good thing. But when you do need help, you need to know that there is nothing wrong if you ask. Not seeking help from others does not necessarily prove your worth as a worker. You are not a phony if you need other's guidance or assistance. A soloist might ask for help, but he will do it in such a way that it sounds as if it is a project requirement, and not because you are having a hard time doing it.

- The expert

The people who belong to this group are afraid of being exposed for not knowing or doing enough. They measure their competence based on the things they can and cannot do and the knowledge they have and do not have. If you are the type of person who will not go for a promotion just because you think you still lack the experience, then you probably belong to this group. You are always trying to improve your skills by getting certifications or attending classes but for you, these are still not enough. You also sometimes find yourself doubting your abilities as a manager for example even if you have been in that position for a long time already.

Although striving to become better and always having the eagerness to learn are good things, you should still not be too hard on yourself. If you cannot take on new roles because you feel you need more certifications, it becomes a form of procrastination. The trick here is to acquire certification or learn new things only when needed. Do not simply "hoard" knowledge or skills just to make yourself feel better and to give yourself a false sense of security.

Keep in mind that impostor syndrome is not a mental disorder but it is just as important to pay attention to the different signs of having an impostor syndrome so that you can address it properly. The training of the Spartans and the Special Operations Forces includes superiors and peers mocking and jeering at them to make them perform even better. And this works because rather than breaking their spirits, the taunts only made them stronger.

On the other hand, if the taunts come from within yourself, it becomes more difficult to handle. They always say that your worst enemy is yourself. But you can still learn a thing or two about how the Spartans and Special Operations soldiers train when it comes to overcoming these negative thoughts about yourself.

To overcome these self-doubts and gain the mindset of a Spartan warrior and a Special Forces soldier, you should continue reading because the next few chapters will teach you more.

3

Fixed and Growth Mindsets

The two basic mindsets—fixed vs growth

Before you learn about the Spartans' and Special Operations Forces' secret to having self-confidence, you first need to understand the two types of mindsets—the fixed mindset and the growth mindset—and which group you belong to.

A fixed mindset is having the belief that everything that you have—your intelligence, personality, skills, character, and abilities—are innate and constant givens. This means that whatever happens to you in life, whether you fail or succeed, is a result of these static traits that you already have since the day you were born. There might be changes as you live your life but these are not significant and do not affect whether you succeed or fail in life.

The other type of mindset, the growth mindset, loves taking on challenges because they see them as a way to grow. Instead of being discouraged when they fail at something, they feel more encouraged to do better because they see it as a challenge. This means that people who have this kind of mindset have a bigger chance of succeeding because failure does not scare them.

You have to understand that the way you behave and your response to unfamiliar situations and new tasks depend on the kind of mindset you have. If two people are offered a promotion but with bigger work responsibilities, one has a fixed mindset and the other has a growth mindset, the first person with the fixed mindset will probably turn down the offer thinking that he may not be able to do it because he does not have the right skills, while the second person will enthusiastically accept even if he lacks the skills because he knows that he can learn them as he goes along.

People who have a fixed mindset always have this belief that they need to prove themselves to others over and over again. Since they believe that their intelligence, personality, and other traits are fixed and inherent, then they feel like others should always see them as intelligent or highly skilled because if they show a deficiency, they think it's the end of them. It is always like a black and white scenario for these people. Either you got it or you don't.

On the other hand we have the growth mindset.People who have a growth mindset believe that the intelligence and traits that you are dealt with in life can still be developed and cultivated. Everything is free-flowing and can still be changed. Just because you were born a certain way does not mean you can change. And because of this mindset, these types of people have higher chances of succeeding in life because they are open to anything. This does not mean that they believe that anyone can be anything they want to be. It does not mean that with enough practice and training, you can be as good as Bach or Mozart even if you do not have any musical affinity whatsoever. It does not mean that you can be as intelligent as Einstein if you study hard. This is not what having a growth mindset means. It means that whatever you already have, you can still cultivate it through the right training and practice until you reach your full potential.

Another main difference between these two mindsets is that while a fixed mindset gets validation from external approval, a growth mindset promotes the willingness to learn. Failure does not equate to not being good but it is viewed as part of the learning process.

For people with a growth mindset, proving yourself to other people over and over again is a big waste of time. You can instead spend this time getting better at something. Instead of pretending that your deficiencies do not exist by doing things you are good at repeatedly just to prove to others that you are good, why not just pay attention to these deficiencies and try to overcome them? Do not just repeatedly do things just because you know you cannot make mistakes since you are already an expert in doing this. Why not challenge yourself and try doing something else that is out of your comfort zone? You might just reveal something about yourself—a hidden talent or a new skill learned.

Another hallmark of the growth mindset is sticking to the task at hand even if it is not going well. The passion and motivation and seeing things through to the end are a part of having a growth mindset. If you know someone who people describe as resilient, a survivor, and thrives even in the most difficult of times, he or she is blessed with a growth mindset. Those tips and advice that go along the lines of 'you can do anything if you put your mind to it' are all part of this willingness to learn and grow.

People with a fixed mindset view risks, difficulties, and efforts as signs of their incompetence and inadequacy. This is why they do not want to put themselves in uncomfortable situations. For them, making an effort is equal to failure. They think that effort is a bad thing and that it is not needed if you are talented or intelligent. In contrast to that people with a growth mindset revere effort. Making an effort is that one thing that helps them acquire a new skill or learn something unfamiliar. In their world, making an effort is the path to success.

The fixed and growth mindsets have been observed even among young children. An experiment was conducted involving a group of four-year-olds. They were given an easy puzzle to solve. After successfully solving the puzzles, they asked the children if they want to re-do the same easy puzzle or move on to a more difficult puzzle. Some children chose to work on the same easy puzzle while others, who thought it was odd to re-do the same puzzle, chose to progress to a more difficult puzzle. This only proved that at a young age, these types of basic mindsets already exist.

You also probably notice how some children in a classroom setting are afraid to raise their hands and ask questions. Some of them may be shy, and that is a different thing. But others are afraid that their teacher and classmates might think that they are stupid because they ask questions.

Another interesting study about these two mindsets was conducted in Columbia. After answering a series of difficult questions, some people only focused on whether their answers are correct or not, and did not pay attention when they were taught how to improve on their mistakes. They already filed these wrong answers as failures. The other subjects, on the other hand, listened intently to information on how they can improve their answers. Their main goal is to do better next time and not only to see if they got all the answers correctly.

There was another experiment conducted regarding these two types of mindset. Two groups of students were given a fairly easy test to answer and all of them got great scored. The first group was praised based on their intelligence—'You got a high score! You are really smart!' The second group was praised based on their effort—'You got a high score! What a hard-working student!' When they were given a choice on which task to do next, the first group immediately picked the ones that are easy because they do not want to make a mistake and they want to keep the positive image that other people have of them. The students in the second group picked more challenging tasks because they were praised for their hard work. And the more challenging the task is, the more work they have to put into it. This also shows that the way people praise others, especially children, affects a person's mindset as he grows older.

As the tasks became harder and more challenging, the students with a fixed mindset were having less and less fun which was the complete opposite of the fun experience that the students with a growth mindset is having. There was also a disturbing discovery when the students were given IQ tests and they were asked to put their scores. A few students who were observed to have a fixed mindset had the tendency to lie. They wrote a score that is higher than what they actually got. This is because they see low scores as deficiencies, which means they are not good enough.

People with a fixed mindset think that success comes from being superior to others in terms of intelligence and talent. On the other hand, people with a growth mindset think that working hard leads to success.

These observations are not only found in classroom or business settings. It can also be seen in personal relationships. Fixed mindset people have an ideal man or woman in mind, a happy-ever-after fairy tale idea of relationships. If their partner falls short or if the relationship does not live up to their sweep-you-off-your-feet expectation, then they will feel disappointed and unhappy. This is why some people cannot be happy in their relationships because they are always looking for someone better who will live up to their expectations. The truth is, this is impossible because a perfect man or woman does not exist. And as they always say, the grass is always greener on the other side.

The key to having a successful relationship is to work hard for it, like what the growth mindset people do. They believe that their relationship is a work in progress. And there is always room for improvement for them and their partner. People who have this kind of mentality are happier and more content with their relationships because they believe that any shortcomings or obstacles can be fixed. These are the people who ride the storm with their partner, who do not automatically think about breaking up or divorcing just because of one mistake. However, just keep in mind that you should also know when to walk away. If the relationship is toxic or abusive, and you have done everything on your part, then maybe it is time to give up. Know the difference between working on a relationship because you know that you have something beautiful, and tolerating or suffering even if the relationship is going nowhere.

Based on these, which kind of mindset do you think the Spartans and the Special Operations Forces have? These extraordinary people have a growth mindset. Of course, most of them probably already have the skills and talents from the day they were born but it helped a lot that they have training that further enhanced their innate abilities.

4

The Mindset of an Elite Spartan Warrior

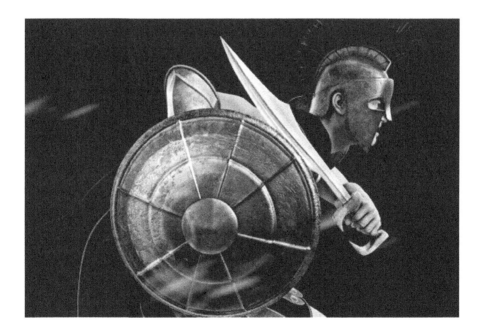

You already know by now the reputation of the Spartan warriors as elite soldiers to be reckoned with. They were dominant and most ancient military forces not only in Greece but also in neighboring countries feared the Spartans. How did these men always come out on top? How did they always achieve victory no matter what the circumstances?

The Spartans had a singular or black-and-white mentality when it came to war—the only goal was to win. Nothing more, nothing less. Even if they did their best and the odds were against their favor, they would still be considered failures by their families and other citizens if they lost. This is why it was unimaginable for a Spartan warrior to lose because they would not only lose the war—they would also lose their purpose of living. Before they went to war, they had to have 100% confidence in their abilities. Self-doubts and second-guessing had no room if they wanted to succeed.

So what kind of preparations did the Spartans do? The following paragraphs will tell you more about the Spartans—how they prepared and their fascinating mindset when it comes to winning. It will surely inspire you to become just like them because they are the kind of people who achieve anything they want no matter what if they put their mind to it.

- Appearance is a powerful self-confidence tool

Sometimes, there are days when you do not feel confident because of the way you look. There are also days when you look in the mirror and you cannot help but think how great you look and it instantly boosts your confidence. Many people say that focusing on your physical appearance is a shallow thing to do and your appearance should not be the basis of your self-confidence. But you cannot deny the fact that physical appearance plays an important role in how you feel about yourself. What makes it negative is when you rely solely on your physical appearance to attain self-confidence.

Let's take a look at the Spartans. If you think they only focused on training and skills, you are wrong because the Spartans also paid close attention to how they looked. They made sure that their reputation as formidable enemies matched how they looked. This helped a lot when it came to intimidating their opponents even before they started their attacks. Just looking at the Spartans would inspire fear and awe among their enemies.

Aside from their physical prowess, Spartans were known to terrorize their enemies with their physical appearance. Before they even took out their weapons, their enemies would start to feel fear not only because the Spartans' reputation preceded them anywhere they went but also because of the way they looked. They wore a scarlet tunic and a cape which they took off before they start fighting. According to historians, the color scarlet was chosen for their battlefield attire because it was the color most suitable for war and was not commonly used in women's clothing. Another theory is that scarlet is the color of blood, and any wound or injury, a sign of weakness, would be well hidden because the blood would just blend in with the clothing. The enemy would not know whether he was inflicting wounds to his Spartan enemy because he would not be able to tell. This would further strengthen their reputation of being formidable because the enemies would say that no matter how much they attacked a Spartan warrior, he did not get easily injured.

The Spartan warriors also took care of their shields and armors, which hung from their arms over the tunic that they wore. Before going to war, they would buff their shield and armor until they gleamed and glisten under the sun. From afar, the enemies would see the brilliant shine of the Spartans' war ensemble.

Another aspect of their appearance that the Spartans paid close attention to was their hair. Long hair had been a popular style in ancient Greece. But when other city-states changed their hairstyles to shorter cuts, the Spartans did not follow the trend and instead kept their hair long. They believed that long hair symbolizes freedom, and they wanted other warriors to see that the Spartans were free men. Moreover, they believed that long hair was beneficial to both handsome and unattractive men. Long hair enhanced a Spartan man's handsome appearance, and at the same time, it made an "ugly" (Plutarch's word) Spartan man more frightful. The elite warriors from Sparta made it a point to always look well-groomed. Their hair was long but it was often braided and they sported beards that they regularly trimmed.

But the most iconic gear that the Spartans had was their helmet. Their helmet became an icon of their prowess even to this day. It was made of bronze and covered the entire face except for the eyes and mouth. On top of the helmet was a horsehair crest that added to their appearance of daunting height. This helmet crowned with horsehair Mohawk gave the illusion that the enemies were not only fighting mere human beings but a machine that could not be quenched and defeated. The dread that the headpiece alone inspired was something that even the most courageous of warriors during the ancient times had experienced.

The Spartans' appearance instilled fear in the enemy even before the war had begun. Then when the enemies had to return home in defeat, they would tell others how formidable the Spartans were even before wielding their weapons. This in turn would further cement their reputation of being the strongest warriors of all.

If you look at it from a modern person's point of view and if you apply it to your own life, you will agree that the way you look has a lot of effect on your self-confidence. For example, if you are going to an interview, wearing an outfit that makes you look like a boss will surely boost your confidence and at the same time will impress your interviewer. Or how wearing red makes a woman feel more confident and seductive than wearing something softer like pink.

· A pre-battle ritual is a must

Did you notice how a lot of successful people have routines that they do unfailingly before they begin their day? Spartans also had to do different kinds of activities before they enter the battlefield. Days leading up to the battle would be filled with physical exercises and further military training and instructions. Breakfast would be sandwiched in between these training but most of the day would be spent doing physical activities including sports competitions. And if you think the Spartans would not pay as much attention to their appearance because they were still preparing, you are wrong because they would still groom their hair, trim their beard, and polish their armor and helmet even during the training. This does not mean that they are vain. This only showed their commitment to always be in their best possible self even when the war had not even begun.

There was even a story that said King Xerxes of Persia ordered a scout to spy on the Spartans before they start the historic battle of Thermopylae. The scout saw the Spartan men grooming their hair and doing some physical exercises without their clothes on. The Spartans believed that fear would creep in if one is idle. It is important to keep busy so that there is no time to talk and to second guess. If you keep going and remain active, you will feel inspired to do more.

In today's world, you have to stay active so that you will not have time to think about negative things. If you are constantly doing something productive, you will forget about your self-doubts and insecurities. At the same time, it hones your skills by practicing every day. It also boosts your mental health by not wallowing on negative things.

· You can be both reverent and fierce

Spartans were known to rely on their skills, physical strength, and mental capabilities but did you know that they were also a society that believed in gods and a force greater than themselves that can further help them to succeed? The Spartans were fearless but not when it comes to their gods. They may look like a group of warriors who were so self-assured they probably did not believe in asking for help from any spiritual beings. And they had every right to solely believe in themselves but they did not.

38

Instead, every time they needed to go to a big event or campaign or even a major battle, they would first consult oracles and make the necessary sacrifices. They pay attention to omens and signs and their decisions were greatly influenced by the censure or sanction of their gods. Young Spartans were taught to fear the gods and this was one of the basic tenets and foundations of the Spartan morals. It may not look like it but the Spartans were pious and it was one of the pillars of their morality and success.

They also valued their religious obligations more than their military duties. That is shocking considering their reputation back then and even up to now but that is the truth. In fact, during the Battle of Marathon, the Spartans delayed the deployment of their warriors because it coincided with a major religious event. The famous King Leonidas also sent only a small group of men to Thermopylae instead of a large force because it was also in the middle of a religious ceremony.

Some would say that this was piety or superstition. Others say it was humility or the acknowledgment that there is a greater force that dictates our fate and that your skills, mental acumen, and talent can only do so much. The gods and spiritual forces still have a much larger and significant influence on your life's successes.

The Spartans believed in themselves and in what they could do but they were also humbled by their belief in a greater force. This is probably why they were such formidable warriors. They were confident but their piety tempered this confidence that helped them make calculated decisions.

You do not necessarily have to believe in a god or a greater force. The major takeaway from this is that having self-confidence is important but acknowledging your limits is just as important.

- To build strength, one must endure

The fighting style during the time of the Spartans was phalanx warfare, which means that the soldiers stood close to each other and fought their enemies side by side. This type of warfare requires stamina, fortitude, and grit much more than speed, cleverness, and agility. The first three terms refer to endurance. If you think about it, endurance was what they needed to succeed in this type of warfare. They needed to be disciplined and committed to reach the end goal. They needed to stand their ground and persevere until the end. They did not necessarily need a lot of the second three groups of traits in phalanx warfare.

This is the main reason why the agoge 's training was built around endurance. The soldiers in training were given meager food, only one piece of clothing, uncomfortable beds made of reed, and many other hardships that they had to endure, not to mention athletic events and physical exercises.

These hardships were not punishment but more as a part of their training. They taught them how to be adaptable and acquire a high tolerance for pain and difficult situations. It was about mental toughness and sticking out until you succeed. The bonus was that it also doubled as physical training. The strength they were talking about here was mental strength. You need mental strength to succeed in life. When under a lot of pressure, your mind and spirit should not easily break. This is also the same thing for confidence. If you know you can do it during the hardest of time, and you know you can endure, it will give you more confidence to face whatever challenge life throws your way. Confidence is gained by persevering and not giving up until you reach your target.

· Less is more

In modern times, the word Sparta is always associated with austerity, frugality, simplicity, and minimalism. In fact, the saying less is more was coined by Chilon, one of the Seven Sages of Greece who came from Sparta. This was the guiding principle of the whole Spartan society—from the clothes they wear and their diet to the words that come out of their mouth. They thought that luxury was a waste of time and resources and it was okay to be a little uncomfortable for the sake of something far greater.

When it comes to speaking, the saying 'less is more' was greatly observed among the Spartans. And today, we use the term 'laconic' to refer to speaking in a few chosen words. When they talked, they made sure that the words were intentional. It would be a waste of energy to just ramble and say a lot of words without really conveying anything. They also believed in short but clever responses. There was one story about Philip II who sent a message to Sparta. He said that if they successfully entered Sparta, he would burn the town down to the ground. And the famous reply he got from the Spartans? "If". Short but sweet and straight to the point. They got their message across for sure. Another story was that of a soldier who fought at Thermopylae. He complained to Leonidas that the Persian soldiers shot so many arrows that the sunlight was temporarily hidden. Leonidas replied that they would then had to battle under the shade.

At first, other Greek city-states thought the Spartans were stupid. But according to Socrates, this was a tactic to mislead enemies into thinking that the Spartans are only physically strong but were intellectually challenged. This is not the case, however, because the Spartans were highly educated people who studied philosophy and language. Just with how they fought during battles wherein they would first aim carefully before releasing their spears, they would also speak and reply in a deliberate manner to ensure that their words hit their mark. Their short and terse words also proved to be beneficial when yelling out commands on the chaotic battlefield. Imagine if your military superior loves verbose and highfalutin statements. You will die first before you hear the end of his order.

The truth is, the Spartans were deliberate speakers because they wanted to make sure that their words would count.This is also true when it comes to developing your self-confidence. When speaking, try not to ramble and be straight to the point. Some people think that the more they say, the more intelligent they are when this is not the case. Do not be afraid of silence if you need to gather your thoughts first before speaking. Do not just automatically say whatever pops in your head. Aside from speaking, you should also avoid relying on material possessions to boost your self-confidence. Acquiring a lot of stuff just because you think it will improve your image is not the right thing to do. Instead, try to get yourself select pieces that are high quality and will last a long time. Anything of high quality will boost your confidence. Plus you will not have the feeling of regret after buying something that you do not need or want.

Less is more also applies to the people around you. You might be surrounded by a lot of "friends" but are they all worth your time and energy? Some might even cause you to have low self-confidence. Surround yourself with positive people who want nothing more than to see you succeed and try to eliminate from your life those who cause you nothing but pain and self-doubt.

· Master your craft

Self-Confidence comes from knowing what you need to do by heart. If you are knowledgeable and skilled in your domain, you will feel confident in performing your tasks and achieving your goal. The Spartans believed in single-minded focus and not losing your sight in doing the thing that you are supposed to do the best way you can. Spartans were known as warriors. They were not expected to farm the land or be involved in trades because other groups of the society were responsible for this. For the elite warriors, they only needed to focus on one thing—and that is to successfully beat enemies that came their way. Their main goal was to become the best warrior of their time.

The Spartans also knew other things. Some of them were sculptors, poets, musicians, dancers, and philosophers. Others excelled in athletic competitions. However, these other cultural endeavors revolved around their ultimate goal—and that was to become the best warrior they could ever be. For them, the highest form of excellence was to master the art of warfare because that is their domain. Ever heard of the saying 'jack of all trades, master of none'? This was something you cannot say about the Spartans because they made it a point to master their domain—all other things were just secondary. Dabbling in warfare was not something you would hear because it was their way of life. Everything was all about winning battles and becoming the best soldiers. They were discouraged from pursuing other crafts such as trades or farming. They were also not allowed to own silver or gold coins because commerce and the desire for wealth would distract them from their ultimate goal. Their craft was warfare. And they were the craftsmen of war.

The main difference between the Spartans and other soldiers was that war was a way of life for the Spartans. Even when there was no war, they still had to train because they were full-time soldiers. Soldiers from other nations would only train for some time, go to war, then go back to whatever it was they were doing, whether they were farmers, tradesmen, or craftsmen. This is why they became the best soldiers not only in their time but also in modern times. A lot of the rules and ethos that modern time soldiers adhere to were based on the Spartans' war tactics and strategies. For most people, one Spartan warrior is equal to several warriors from other city-states. That's how great they were in what they do.

You can become more confident if you are an expert in what you do. Be more like the Spartans. When they have a goal, they put their whole heart into achieving this goal. And the results were phenomenal. Anything half baked or dabbling into something just won't do. You have to work on it full time if you want to have the kind of confidence that will lead you to succeed.

- Learn to fight from habit

It is safe to say that fighting in war and training for it was the habit of a Spartan soldier. From the day they were born and teenage years, to adulthood and old age, a Spartan's life was all about fighting in a war. This is why fighting became more like a habit for them. It was just like a part of their life's many routines. Like how modern men go to work every day to earn a living. The art of warfare was instilled in them from a very young age. It was a part of their being. Imagine training for war hundreds of times more than an average Greek soldier. Fighting was second nature to these elite warriors. What made them lose their fear of the unknown circumstances of war was their familiarity with it. After all, they had been training for it all their life. And seasonal soldiers would feel discomfort and fear because they were not used to it. They were not as prepared as their Laconic counterparts. They knew that there would be hardships but their preparations were not enough, unlike the Spartans whose training was probably more difficult than the actual battle itself.

Instead, these seasonal soldiers fight from their emotions. They would psyche themselves up and tell themselves that they could do it. They would boost each other's morale but at the end of the day, fighting from habit would beat fighting from feeling hands down. A person who grew up eating meat will be more willing to try meat byproducts such as intestines than a person who grew up vegetarian. The analogy is a little off topic but it shows that growing up with something will make it easier for you to deal with it later on in life than if you just encountered it recently or for the first time.

If you are going to apply this to building self-confidence, it only tells you that you have to need to form a habit out of it if you want to be confident while doing it. If you want to be a confident person in general, just try to always challenge yourself doing unfamiliar things, and pretty soon, you will not find it difficult to accept new challenges in life and you will have more confidence doing new things.

Now that you know the secrets of the formidable Spartan soldiers, you should now have a look at the kind of mindset that Special Operations forces have.

5

The Mindset of a Special Operations Soldier

The closest modern counterpart of the Spartans is probably the Special Operations forces. These people are trained not only to fight but to perform special operations tasks that are not included in the responsibility of a regular soldier such as counter-terrorism, infiltration, espionage, and so on. A member of any Special Operations unit should have the right mindset if they want to succeed in their tasks. Here are some of the things that you should try if you want to have the mindset of an elite soldier.

· Turn on your survival mode

If you know that what you need to do is a matter of life or death, you will have a greater motivation to succeed. Elite soldiers are usually faced with decisions that will either make them live or die. Sometimes, it is even worse because they have to think not only for their own good but for the good of their team, or even a whole nation. Sometimes, their actions and decisions will affect the fate of the whole world even. This is why there is no room for second-guessing yourself if you are a part of this elite team. When you are driving and the car in front of you suddenly stopped without warning, you do not have the luxury of time to think about whether to swerve or to put on the break. You just have to confidently follow your first gut instinct because deciding to swerve to either left or right, then changing your mind a split second later to put on the breaks instead can cause even more accidents.

You can apply this to your journey to achieving self-confidence. If you know that you need the confidence to survive in this dog-eat-dog world, then you will try your best to build your confidence. If you know that the roof over your head and the food on your plate depend on you accepting new tasks with bigger responsibilities, then you will muster everything you have to get that confidence you need. If you know your family depends on you, and all you need to do is to have the confidence to try, then you will have a bigger motivation to go for it. It is just having the right mindset and thinking that you need your self-confidence to survive that will do the trick.

· Always have an escape plan

This is one of the things that they teach Special Operations forces—always search for a possible escape plan when going somewhere, especially if it is an enemy's territory. These elite soldiers are almost always in situations that require an escape plan. This is why when they plan an attack they always study the area or building first. They will check the entry and exit points and will look for an escape route that they can take especially if things do not go according to plan. Whether they find themselves in a familiar place like a local Starbucks or a government office somewhere in Afghanistan, they will make sure that they know where to go when things go bad.

This is also true when it comes to building the right mindset for success. It is like having a plan B. For example, if you decide to put a huge chunk of your savings in business, you should have a plan B just in case the business does not succeed. It is like an insurance that will give you not only confidence but also peace of mind. You might want to leave a small part of your savings untouched or you can ask your parents to lend you money beforehand in case your business fails. Escape plans give you confidence because you know that no matter what happens, you will have a fallback or something that you can work on again from scratch.

· Start your day early

Have you ever heard of someone telling you to start your day in the afternoon if you want to succeed in life? The most common advice given not only by the Special Operations units but also life coaches and successful people is to start your day early. The early bird catches the worm and all that stuff. You need to start your day early so that you will accomplish so much more. Moreover, almost every business opens in the morning. You will be able to finish everything you need to do on time and you might still have extra time to do other things because you already finished what you had to do. Waking up before everyone else does gives you a peaceful feeling and the energy to start and finish on time. Military men often wake up early to exercise because nothing beats jogging just when the sun is about to rise, breathing in that fresh air, and hearing the sound of the birds chirping. Although exercising is the best activity in the morning, you can also try other things such as journaling, gardening, or just having early morning breakfast.

Try to pay attention to your day when you wake up early. You will notice that you are more productive and you accomplish so much more than if you wake up late. This makes you more confident with how your day is going to unfold because you already have an early start. Knowing that you still have plenty of time to finish what you have to do makes you feel more confident. Procrastination has no room when it comes to building your self-confidence because you will only feel rattled knowing that your deadline is almost done but you still have a lot of stuff to do.

- Trust your gut

Soldiers who fight overseas almost always use their instinct when it comes to making decisions. If they do not feel good about a certain place or situation, they will try to avoid it by not walking into it. There is no logical explanation for this but you better listen to what your gut feeling is telling you. More often than not, it is correct and this has saved so many lives a lot of times. Soldiers would feel weird about a certain area then they would not go through it and they will instead find an alternate route. Later on, they would find out that a convoy got ambushed by unknown attackers.

Whatever it is, it is your intuition telling yourself that you are in danger and that you should try a different way. You need to learn how to confidently trust your gut. After all, this is yourself and yourself is telling you that something is weird. This means that you need to have to trust yourself when making decisions. It cannot be explained by reason but trusting your gut and confidently following what it is telling you can lead you to success. Some say intuition is your wisdom from years of experiences telling you what needs to be done. Gut feeling has always been there since you were a child but the kind of dilemmas that you have as an adult are of course more serious and affect your life in general.

- Learn how to read people

You cannot be confident if you do not know who you are dealing with. Remember that more often than not, you do not feel confident because you are unfamiliar with the situation. In this case, you do not know what you are up against. One piece of advice given by a Special Forces soldier is to always be suspicious with people around you, even your operations partner. This always keeps them on their toes. A person who always automatically agrees to everything you say looks suspicious. He must be either really stupid or is desperate to be on your good side. Either way is not good for your team.

It is important to know if a person is genuine or has an ulterior motive. This way, you will be able to respond appropriately and confidently. You do not need to have the powers of a psychic to be able to understand people. Just pay close attention and be mindful of the way they talk and behave.

Another way that you can apply this to your journey to building self-confidence is when you need to know the kind of people you work with. If you have a presentation in front of your bosses, you need to understand the things that your bosses will look for in your presentation. By knowing what they want to see, you can better prepare for your report and you will be more comfortable when talking in front of them because you know that you are giving them the information that they are looking for. This is the same way when you are applying for a job. Learn the company's background and the kind of work that they do so that you have an idea of what you are getting yourself into.

· Look the part

The Spartans also believed in taking care of their appearance to instill fear in their enemies and also to make themselves feel more confident. Special Ops people also do the same thing. Military men, whether working in Special Operations units or regular units, are known for being impeccably dressed and groomed. You might see Special Ops men being casual and sporting a 12 o'clock shadow or an unkempt hair but they only do this when they need to blend in with the crowd or when they need to go undercover. Otherwise, they will not be able to accomplish their undercover tasks.

The way the Spartans dressed and groomed themselves might be completely different from how the soldiers today take care of their physical appearance but the idea is the same—the way they look is important to tackle any tasks successfully.

In combat zones, these elite soldiers always try to make themselves well-groomed and clean-shaven as the circumstances allow. Their uniform and weapons are clean, well-maintained, and always in order. Sometimes, the training makes them feel like wild animals but they are still expected to have good hygiene. Brushing their teeth in the morning instantly boosts their morale by up to 13%.

You should also learn to pay attention to your clothes. You do not need to be as neat and orderly as the military but at least try to iron your wrinkly clothes, wear clothes that are your size, and always make sure that you are presentable. Looking confident will make you feel more confident about yourself.

· Work out a battle plan

You very well know that the military does not just attack whenever they feel like it. It is a complicated affair that requires a lot of careful planning. Before going to the battlefield, they prepare everything—from the weapons that they need to use and the number of men that they need to deploy to surveying the area and checking for escape plans. There are so many things that they need to plan and even emergency attacks have some kind of a loose plan. They also have plans in different possible scenarios.

This is applicable in your everyday life. Mapping out your goals and listing down everything you need to accomplish at a certain time will make it easier for you to achieve your goals on or before the deadline. For example, if you need to submit a financial report for the whole month of February by the end of the week, you need to make sure that everything is planned. Maybe try to finish the first two weeks on the first day, then the last two weeks on the second day. This will give you plenty of time to tweak and finalize everything and also to practice in case you need to present it to your boss.

By having a list of the things that you need to do, you will feel more confident because you already have a plan that will help you accomplish everything you need to do for the day and before the deadline.

• Focus

In the Special Ops units, they always have a target that they need to achieve using one of their many skills and knowledge. It is important to stay focused on this target and not get distracted by other things. On the battlefield, the soldiers have to stay focused on their goal otherwise they will find themselves in a difficult situation. If your goal is to walk west for an hour to reach your destination, you need to focus on that and not get distracted by other things that you see along the road.

This is also true when it comes to your life right now. If you have a long-term goal, always keep your eyes on your goal so that you will not get distracted. If your goal is to earn 20% of your savings every month so that you will be able to afford a house in a couple of years, you need to stay strong and not get tempted by all the sales and promotions that you receive in your emails and texts. Even if you go out with your friends, resist the temptation to buy things that you do not need and instead always remind yourself why you need to save money. Always tell yourself that in the future, you will have a house that you can call your own and you will no longer need to rent and share with roommates. Try to remember why you are doing these sacrifices so that it will keep you motivated and you will not lose track of what you want to achieve.

How to Become a Confident Leader

Special Operations soldiers have to undergo leadership training because they will most likely find themselves in a leadership position many times in their career. Whether it is a two-man team or a whole battalion, a leader must lead with confidence. There are only two types of leaders in any setting—whether it is military, corporate, or government—effective and ineffective. If you are an effective leader, you can drive your team forward to your goals using fair and reasonable practices. If you are ineffective, you lack the ability to push the whole team to achieve your target. Every leader wants to be an effective leader. And if you are aiming for a leadership position in your company or anywhere else in your life, you should check out the next few paragraphs.

- Authority

You might think this is obvious but you would not believe the number of leaders who do not exercise authority over their team. Having authority does not mean that you need to be the best and the most knowledgeable or skilled in your team, although it will help if the leader is highly skilled and knowledgeable. Authority is something that cannot be demanded or learned. Like trust, it is earned. A leader earns it after exhibiting good judgment by making sound decisions and dependability in front of his peers. It might sound easy to build authority but it takes a lot of time and experience with the team.

You need to be a reassuring presence when things get bad. You should be the first one they seek for advice when they need it. Your team should look up to you for guidance. This is why a leader should lead by example if he wants to build authority over his team. If you lead by example, the team members will follow even without being told. As a leader, you need to learn to listen to your team members and have accountability. Nothing is worse than a member who will blame everything on his subordinates even if it is his fault. As a leader, it is important that you keep your eyes on your team's goals and always give them wisdom and strength that will make them trust and depend on you.

- Empathy

Another skill that you should master to have confidence in any leadership position is empathy. This is probably the most complicated and difficult part of being a leader. Although you have to keep your eyes focused on your team's goal, you should also not forget to look around you and pay attention to your team members who are the driving force behind your initiatives. It is not advisable to be best friends with any of your team members because it can get messy but you should strive to become an ear who would listen to what they have to say. Maybe talk to your team one by one and just try to catch up on their lives. At least know a little bit about them, whether or not they are married, how many family members they have, where they live, and so on.

You can also organize team buildings at least once a month as a way to get to know your team outside of work. Knowing a little bit about them will at least give you an insight into the things that motivate them, their inspiration, and other details that can help you achieve your goals. It may sound like you are just trying to get to know them personally just to reach your goal but that should not be the case. Be genuinely interested in your team and build a great relationship with them. Make them feel that they can approach you anytime if something is bothering them.

Empathy makes your team put their trust in you. It does not mean that you are showing them a weak or soft side and that this could negatively affect your authority over them. This is why you need to know the right combination of authority and empathy, of being their leader and their friend at the same time.

· Body language

To be confident in communicating with your team, you have to pay close attention to your body language. Did you know that words are just 7% of communication and the rest is your body language and tone of your voice? Words are meaningless if not backed by the right body language and tone. Imagine if you are saying 'I love you' to someone, but in a monotonous way and your hands are just hanging limply on your side while your eyes are looking anywhere but at the person you are saying the words to? It is the same when it comes to communicating with your team as their leader.

When talking, always keep your hands out of your pockets. Do not cross your arms in front of you. Use your hands while talking. It will show that you are animated and passionate about what you are talking about. Do not slouch when talking, whether you are standing or sitting. This will give the illusion of stature, like what the Spartans did. Make eye contact with your audience when you are talking to them, no matter how small or big the crowd is. If there are hundreds of people in front of you, try to make eye contact with the ones near you but do not forget to look towards the end even if you know eye contact is impossible. At least they know that you acknowledge them.

- Sincerity

Being sincere is one of the things that you need to do if you want to gain your team's trust. Insincerity can be linked to dishonesty. Do not give your team false motivations just to make them do what you want them to do. You have to be genuine with what you tell them because this will all eventually come back to you. When you say you want them to do well, be sure you mean it with your heart. Do not be a leader who just fakes caring about his subordinates. Be mindful of what comes out of your mouth. Because once you make a mistake and you are exposed as being insincere, your team will not trust you again. Trust is difficult to gain back once broken, no matter how small the issue is. If you are sincere about your intentions and what you want to achieve, everything else will follow, including having a great relationship with your team and leading them with confidence.

6

Overcoming Fear to Gain Self-Confidence

Did you know that the biggest obstacle in having self-confidence is fear? There are instances when you know what you need to do but you are too afraid to try. Ask anyone you know and they most likely have at least one thing that they are scared of doing. It does not have to be a phobia. It could be something like fear of commitment, relationships, public speaking, trying new things, or failure. In some cases, these fears are caused by your past experiences. Maybe in the past, you had been hurt by your long-term partner who makes you not want to commit to a serious relationship. Or maybe you completely blanked out while speaking in public for the first time in your life and you do not want to experience the same thing again. However, there are instances when these fears are illogical. Sometimes, you are just scared to do something for no particular reason. Your mind just tells you that you cannot do it and you believe it, even if it is not true.

But you have to remember that the feeling of fear is real. It is not an illusion that you can easily ignore. Even the bravest men in the world experience fear at one point or another in their lives. It only becomes detrimental when this fear is unreasonably magnified and it becomes the only thing that fills your head. Instead of focusing on what you can do, you let fear take control of your life and this keeps you from doing things.

Special Ops guys are often faced with fear. They also experience panic or the fight or flight dilemma. Panic keeps them from thinking clearly. And this is a big no-no when they are on a mission because it can mean life or death. But for these guys, they do not allow fear to master them because then they will not be able to accomplish their missions. So what do you need to do to overcome fear and gain self-confidence to do things?

· Use your fear to your advantage

It may sound impossible to do but this is what most military men do. If they look at fear as something they need to evade and escape from, they will find themselves in even worse situations because it is something that you cannot escape from. Like what was mentioned earlier, fear is real. And the thing that you are afraid of is real. Whether it is a major job interview, a large credit card bill, or a big life decision that you have to make, it exists and you have to face it sooner or later. Remember the movie Confessions of a Shopaholic? The lead actress always keeps her credit card bills in her drawer, unopened. She does not want to look at them as if her debts will go away if she ignores them. Eventually, she realized that she has to be an adult and face her problems by going to the bank and talking to them. This is how you should handle fear. Face it head-on. And how are you going to use it to your advantage, you might ask. You are probably obsessing over your problem already, so use the information and scenarios that you have built up in your head in coming up with a solution to your fear. Look at it in a positive light.

For example, if you are afraid to speak in public because you know for a fact that you will be speaking in front of hundreds of people, you can use this information when you visualize yourself speaking in public. Tell yourself, so there will be hundreds of people. How will I address them and make them feel like I am talking to each one of them? Eye contact is possible only for the ones in front but I will still try to look at the back or maybe ask questions addressed to the back of the room. You can use the details that you are already obsessing about but in a positive way.

· Prepare for worst-case scenarios

The key to overcoming fear is preparation, as you probably already know by now after reading the first few chapters of this book. Special Ops soldiers were taught to come up with different worst-case scenarios and find ways on how to overcome these. They are taught to rehearse for adversity so that when the actual adversity does happen, they would know what to do. You might think this is counter-intuitive, focusing on worst-case scenarios when you are trying to overcome fear. But this is helpful because at least you are using your mind to come up with solutions instead of simply telling yourself that you cannot do it.

Michael Phelps' goggles flooded while swimming at the Olympics and he could not see at all. But he rehearsed the scenario so many times so even if his goggles were flooded, he just counted the number of strokes and did his flip turn at the perfect time. And he won. You can apply this in your everyday life. If you have a job interview, you should prepare not only for the questions that interviewers usually ask but also issues that might come up, like when you are asked a question you genuinely do not know the answer to. Maybe your solution is to just be honest about it but tell the interviewer that you are willing to learn. Having a contingency plan in place makes you feel more confident about the thing that you are supposed to do.

· Do not stray too far from your comfort zone

You always hear people tell you that you should go out of your comfort zone if you want to succeed in life. Fair enough. That is sound advice that everyone should follow. If you just stay inside your comfort zone all the time, you will not experience new things and you will not grow as a person. However, you should also know the extent to which it is still considered productive to go. If you work in a corporate setting and you suddenly feel like you want a change of environment, do not decide to become a painter, especially if you do not have any talent from the beginning. This is way out of your comfort zone and is not practical and realistic at all. Maybe you can try painting as a hobby but not as a career. If you want to change jobs and work in a more creative setting, maybe you can apply as a manager of a museum or art gallery. It is still out of your comfort zone but not too far from it that it is not realistic any more. But after mastering that area that challenges you, maybe the next area is not so impractical anymore. Now that you are working in an art gallery, maybe you already started painting as a hobby and you learned a lot from the artists and art around you. Maybe being a painter is not too far off. Keep pushing yourself because you will never know your limits until you reach them.

Remember that comfort zone is that area in your life where you feel most comfortable and because you are comfortable, you do not have any challenges and you do not grow as an individual. Outside the comfort zone are the things that are challenging and help you increase your self-confidence. And beyond this area are things that are not practical and realistic anymore. Learn these areas in your life so you would know up until when you should push yourself.

· Complete safety is an illusion

You need to understand that 100% safety is an illusion. If this is all you ever think about, you will not risk anything and you will live a life without any challenges. It is like aiming for perfection. No one and nothing is perfect and no matter how safe, it is still not entirely safe. If you keep pursuing these impossible goals, then you will not live life. You need to embrace risks and challenges and look at them as part of growing as an individual.

This is why when an opportunity arises you need to seize it right away. Do not wait for yourself to be 100% prepared because you can never fully prepare for anything. Although preparing for marriage and having kids is important, you should not wait too long because you can never fully prepare for these kinds of things. There will be problems and challenges and it is okay because they are part of life.

If you keep on preparing, you might end up not trying at all. You might be missing out on some of the best opportunities and experiences of your life because there is always that feeling that you still have not done enough preparation. Keep in mind that being ready does not mean that your plan of action is 100% foolproof or that uncertainty is completely absent. It only means that you prepared for it as much as you can and the next step would be to try.

· Time is ticking

Consistently remind yourself that you only have one life and time is continuously ticking. It will not wait for you to overcome your fear. Treat every day of your life as if it is your last and you will find yourself doing things that you will not do if you know you have plenty of time to ponder and mull it over in your head. Grab that opportunity. Take that first step. What matters is the here and the now. If tomorrow does not come, at least you have lived a full life.

· Inject humor

Humor solves a lot of problems and laughing it off when you feel fear creeping in is a great way to make light of the situation. Sometimes, you take things too seriously without realizing it when you could be having fun. In scary movies, there is usually that one guy in the group who cracks jokes when things get serious and you can see that it instantly eases the tension. If you feel afraid of doing something, you should make a joke out of it. If you are in an important meeting with your bosses, and you can feel yourself shaking and sweating, you can crack a joke to make the mood lighter. Maybe tell them something like, 'with the way I am shaking and sweating, you would think I'm going to propose to all of you!' You have seen this in a lot of speeches like in Oscars even in the President's public address. Humor makes things less serious and a lot easier to handle. It also instantly builds rapport and camaraderie between you and the people you are interacting with. Tell yourself that things are going to be okay and you are worrying over nothing.

· Ignore that negative little voice in your head

Remember that this voice in your head that tells you negative things, that you cannot do it, that you are not good enough, that is also you. You are your worst enemy. When you are in a situation and you start hearing this tiny voice in your head that puts you down, tell him to shut up. The truth is that the kind of voice that you hear represents how you view yourself. If the voice tells you negative things about yourself, it only means that you do not have confidence in yourself. If it is a voice that boosts you up, then you are on the right track because you already have the confidence that everyone needs. But you will not be reading this book in the first place if you already have confidence, so most likely you are hearing the negative voice. Deal with it by ignoring the voice and slowly but surely replacing it with the more positive one.

· Talk about your fear

If you keep your fear all bottled up inside, it will have a more lasting effect and might come out in the worst possible time. You need to deal with your fear as and when you feel it. Do not allow it to take its root in your mind until it consumes you. Soldiers are being taught to discuss their fear with mental health practitioners. This allows them to process what will happen or what had already transpired. More often than not, keeping their traumas bottled up inside only affects their relationships with their loved ones.

If you feel afraid of doing something, you should not pretend that you are not scared at all. It also does not necessarily mean that you go directly to a therapist to talk. You can just tell a close friend or a loved one about what you are feeling and why you are feeling that way. Sometimes, when you say it out loud, it leaves your thoughts and it allows you to face your fear right away. It is also important to identify your fear. Give it a name. Not Sarah or Michael. Specify what it is exactly you are afraid of. Say something like, I am afraid to speak in public or I am scared to move to a different state. If you ignore your fear, it only grows inside you like a big monster. But if you face it head-on, it becomes smaller and easier to crush.

· Think about the future

The future is a big unknown and a lot of people fear the future because they do not know what is in store for them. This is why you need to think long-term when it comes to facing your future. For instance, if you are afraid that your income will not be enough for your future kids, you should start doing something about it to alleviate this fear of the unknown future. Maybe you can find another job that pays better or start a business or sideline. You can then use the money to save up. It is a long-term plan but at least it makes you feel a little less scared and more confident in your ability to start a family and raise your own kids.

· Educate yourself

It has been said many times that fear comes from the unknown. This is why it is important to learn more about the thing that scares you. If you are a non-native English speaker and you are planning to take an English test and you feel scared that you will not pass, instead of wallowing in your fear, why not study and learn how the exam works? Arm yourself with facts rather than speculation and guesses and you will see that your fear is often baseless.

These are the things that you need to do to overcome fear and gain self-confidence. Most of the information in this book is about gaining self-confidence by overcoming fear. Because fear is the biggest obstacle that you have to overcome to be confident in everything that you do.

7

Mental and Emotional Toughness

Now that you know how the Spartans and Special Operations forces trained to achieve that level of confidence, you should now learn a few more techniques and tips that you can use in your everyday life, whether it is for your personal or work needs.

Caring for Your Physical, Emotional, and Mental Health

Taking care of your body is probably the easiest thing to do, although many people still neglect to do it. You need a balanced diet, do regular exercise, and get enough sleep every day. What about your emotional and mental health? Did you know that your mental and emotional health also affects your physical health? There is a physical manifestation such as high blood pressure, chest pain, and ulcers if you don't take care of your mental and emotional health properly. Do not allow it to come to this and read the following tips on how to care for your mental and emotional health.

· Boost your support system

You have to strengthen your circle of friends who will be there to support you when you need it. This does not necessarily mean that you have to be friends with more people. According to the Spartans, minimalism is the key to success and you should eliminate the ones that you do not need. It means that you should focus more on the quality of your friendships than quantity. Just maintain friendship with the ones that are genuinely your friends. Friendship goes both ways. These are people who you know will be there for you through hell and high waters, and you know in your heart that you will also do the same.

· Learn about your mental and emotional health

It was only in recent years when people started paying attention to their emotional and mental health. Before, it was always about physical health. If you look at the training of Special Ops units, they now have something for improving mental health. These people perform high-risk tasks and experience mental traumas and their mental health must be at its optimal condition. You need to learn more about it. If you are suffering from anxiety, you need to learn more about the different causes and triggers. The more you know, the less you will be afraid, and the more confident you will be.

• Be active

Like what you learned about the Spartans, they did not like being idle, even when they were not preparing for war. Doing some physical exercises every day keeps the blood flowing and keeps you from thinking about negative things. If you are under medication or even you do not need medication but you have mild depression, regular exercise is a good partner and can help a lot. It is also a great way to clear your head. You see this all the time in the movies. The lead characters are fighting and one of them will go out for a run to clear his head. When he comes back, he would be in a better mood because he was able to think things through.

• Start a new hobby

This is more than just learning a new skill or talent. It is about igniting that passion that you have in you. Look at the people who invest time and effort in doing things that they love. They look happy and passionate. Find something that you love to do. It can be something as simple as taking up gardening or collecting antiques, or something a little more expensive like traveling or doing extreme sports. If you have a hobby, your mind will always be busy doing things that you love. The thing about depression is that they lose the passion, that spark that brings joy. You should not only ignite that spark but keep it burning all the time by investing in your passion.

• Always do things in moderation

The Spartan way is to be as minimalist as possible, but if it is too much for you, you can just do things in moderation. Anything done in excess is bad. It is important to eat healthy but eating out or eating anything that makes you happy, as long as you do it in moderation, is also good for your mental and emotional health. Eating a salad every day can be depressing, so make yourself happy by eating a slice of cake from time to time. Getting drunk was frowned upon by the Spartans and the Special Operations forces. However, drinking alcohol in moderation is just fine. As long as you can handle yourself and you are not going to regret it later, then it's okay.

· Do yoga and meditation

This is for stress management. Meditation makes you more mindful of your thoughts. It helps alleviate negative thoughts that can ultimately lead to depression. Yoga is both physical and mental. It makes you more flexible but at the same time, it teaches mindfulness. You can also try deep breathing that will help you calm down if you are experiencing a panic attack. This makes you more in tune with your mind and body and will make you feel more confident about yourself.

· List down your goals

Whether it is your daily list of things to do or your long-term goals, it is a great idea to have a list because it will help you manage your time properly. You can set a deadline for your goals so that you can better manage your time wisely. This makes you more productive and you can set aside time for other things like your hobby or you can spend more time with your loved ones. It will also give you that sense of accomplishment every time you tick a goal that you have finished. This helps reduce your stress from panicking because everything is planned out carefully.

· Set limits

This is another thing that makes you feel exhausted. You should learn how to say no especially if it is not your job or if you do not want to do it. You should also learn how not to bite more than you can chew. Set your limits and also know what your limits are. If your boss is asking you to extend again, you need to learn how to say no. There is a way of saying no without being too blunt and rude about it. You can do it in a nice but firm way.

Keep in mind that learning how to take care of your mental and emotional well being is just as important as physical health. This makes it easier for you to handle stress and anything that life throws at you. Keep in mind, though, that you need to seek professional help if your issues are more serious.

Build Confidence through Mental Toughness like the Navy SEALS

The Navy SEALS is one of the most famous Special Ops groups in the world. They are known for their toughness and expertise in handling high-risk operations. They are some of the toughest men in the world. And it would make sense to get advice from them when it comes to mental toughness and self-confidence.

The training of the Navy SEAL is a lot more than physical training but also exercises to achieve mental toughness. Here are some useful tricks that the Navy SEALS use for mental resilience.

- Practice segmentation

It is just a fancy term for facing a daunting task one manageable step at a time. It has been said many times before but only because it works. Sometimes, you become too overwhelmed by a big project and you feel paralyzed and you cannot start at all. This is because you are looking at it from the wrong perspective. Look at the task at hand as tiny, little tasks that you need to do at a certain time. For example, if you need to clean your whole house before your parents arrive by the end of the week, you might feel overwhelmed. You can instead break it down into smaller tasks. On the first day, start with the living room, then move to the kitchen on the second day, and so on, until you reached your ultimate goal. If you compartmentalize the tasks into smaller ones, you will have more confidence in achieving your goal.

- Try visualization

Visualization is another technique that they teach to people who want to be more confident. There was a study among basketball players, wherein one group practiced free throws for real and another group just visualized it. The results were surprising. The first group scored 24% higher while the second group scored 23% higher. It shows that the difference is not that much, only 1%. Imagine what you can achieve if you combine your actual practice with visualization.

There are techniques on how you should visualize your goals. First, it should be detailed. To do this, you have to visualize using all your senses. This will make it as vivid and as real as possible. Next, you should do it again and again. Repetition is like practicing every day. You also turn it into a habit or something that is familiar. You are not allowed to think about failing. You should always see yourself accomplishing your goals. Finally, imagine the consequences if you fail. Maybe your family and friends will be disappointed. Or maybe you will not be able to buy that house for your family that you promised them. This will give you even more motivation to succeed.

· Do the 4 by 4

The Navy SEALS has a simple solution to instantly staying calm and collected. They call it the 4 by 4 which includes inhaling for 4 seconds, exhaling for 4 seconds, and repeating the entire process for 4 minutes. This is a yoga breathing exercise for body relaxation and is an age-old approach to instantly relieving stress and nerves. When you are under a lot of stress, your body releases cortisol, adrenaline, and norepinephrine. These are hormones that instantly give you that much-needed focus and boost of energy. However, high levels of these hormones make you nervous and on edge. This is why you sometimes have trouble sleeping and cannot relax. This makes you feel even more stressed that can in turn affects your immune system. Doing the 4 by 4 can help you feel more calm and relaxed. If you are in your most relaxed state, you will feel more confident. This is also a form of meditation that allows you to just be at peace with yourself.

· Practice Reframing

You always hear people tell you that you cannot change others but you can change yourself or what you believe in. This is called reframing or non-reactivity. You do not react to negative external stimuli but instead, you change how you think about it. The Navy SEALS have to undergo physical training and tests for mental toughness. The sergeant will intentionally belittle them and tell them negative things to break their spirit. If you believe what the trainer is saying, you will give up and quit right then and there. If you frame it in your mind and tell yourself that it is just part of the training and it is not the truth, you will pass the test with flying colors. In real life, you can turn negative events into something positive. If someone in your office is being petty and mean, instead of thinking that the person does not like you and wallowing in self-pity, just tell yourself that she does not know you and you should not be affected by it. The coworker will eventually get tired because she is not getting any reaction from you. By doing this, you are teaching yourself to be calm and positive even when there are negative outside events.

· Celebrate small positives

Everyone had his or her own share of bad days. You did not wake up to your alarm, there was heavy traffic on your way to work, you were late, your boss was not in a good mood, your girlfriend was mad at you because you forgot that it was your anniversary, you forgot your wallet, etc. So many negative things can happen in one day. And these kinds of things happen. It is not just in the movies. Instead of getting frustrated because everything is going wrong, why not find the silver lining? Any situation always has a silver lining. You did not wake up to your alarm; at least you had a good sleep. There was an accident that's why there was a traffic jam; at least you were not hurt. Your girlfriend was mad at you; you can make it up to her by taking her out to a fancy (and relaxing) dinner which you both need. These small victories are often ignored especially when there are just so many wrong things happening. By celebrating and focusing on these small victories, you are creating a cycle of positivity in your life.

· Be someone whom others need

One way to instantly boost your confidence is to know that you are needed. For some people, hardships are just parts of life that they need to overcome. What is more difficult is not being needed, as if you are dispensable. This is why you need to surround yourself with people who need you but at the same time, they provide the support that you also need. Your tribe should be built upon mutual respect, support, trust, and dependency. If it is just one way, and you are the one who always gives without getting anything in return, you will feel burnt out. This gives you a kind of purpose; it gives your life meaning in this world that often offers meaningless conversations, relationships, and possessions. Your group of people should share the same principles and vision in life if you are going to experience the toughest of times with them.

8

Take Action

Turn Yourself into an Action Taker from a Mere Passive Observer

There are also actions that you need to take to become a confident individual who is successful in life. There are so many sayings that place value on taking action. Action speaks louder than words. Walk your talk. Practice what you preach. This is because the action will lead you to the success that you are craving. It is not only about changing the way you think or feel. The driving force behind everything in this world is action. Unless you get up and start your day, your day will not happen, will it? Some people are afraid to take action because they are afraid to fail. They would rather not do anything than take action and fail. But ask yourself, what if you succeed? It is a 50-50 chance.

The Spartans were always active because they understood the importance of taking action and how being idle gave room to negative thoughts like fear and self-doubt. Stop being an observer of other people's success and start taking action. Studying about the Spartans and the Special Operations units will not do you any good if all you will ever do is study. Put everything into action and you will see how far you will go.

· Stop over-thinking

This is easier said than done, especially for some people who have the tendency to think about things that happened even years ago. If you have made mistakes in the past, snap out of it and focus on the present. Although learning from the past is a good thing, overanalyzing past mistakes until you become paralyzed with fear will prevent you from taking action. To be confident in taking the first step towards doing something new and different, you have to move on from the past. Just chalk your past mistakes up to experience and you would be good to go. When you find yourself remembering the past and you start doubting yourself, just breathe deeply for a few minutes and stay in the moment. Tell yourself that it is all in the past and you are starting anew. Once you do this, you will find it easier to take action. Just imagine the kind of past mistakes that the Special Ops soldiers have to move past. It must be difficult for them but they are still able to do it.

· Tell people about your goals

How many times have you told yourself that you will lose weight but you always end up not doing it anyway? But if you tell other people about it, you will feel more committed to your goal because you do not want to disappoint them or you will feel embarrassed about giving up. You do not want them to see you as a failure, especially if it is something as simple as losing weight. Aside from giving you accountability, telling your loved ones about your goals is also a form of motivation. They will be there to support you and build up your confidence in achieving your target weight. They might even join you in your journey to a healthier you. Your loved one can also remind you about what you have already done whenever your motivation is low so that you will not give up. It is even better if you are doing the same thing for them.

· Hold yourself accountable

Although it is nice to have someone who will be there to support you and boost your motivation and confidence, you should still find a way to learn how to hold yourself accountable even without the help of others. This is one ultimate sign of maturity, self-discipline, and self-confidence. You should know what needs to be done by setting standards and goals for yourself. In the long run, this is the best thing to do because you are not relying on another person to help you achieve your goal. This will also test your self-confidence when it comes to achieving things by yourself at your own pace and your own accord. But before you do this, you have to be 100% sure that you will not slack off and make excuses for yourself. You might give yourself excuses without realizing it and before you know it, you just end up not accomplishing anything. So be careful before you try this.

· Keep it simple

Sometimes, you tend to make things more complicated than they actually are. If they ask you to solve 2+2, do not make it more complicated by writing 2(1x2). It is a simple problem that requires a simple solution. For example, if your boss asked you to create a productivity report by comparing current and previous months, do not be too excited that you end up researching the past five years' productivity. Being proactive in the workplace is encouraged but if it is not necessary, then there is no need to do it. To be proactive, maybe you can just give a prediction for the next month's productivity.

· Pay attention to the process

Instead of focusing on the obstacles that might come your way, why not just focus on the process and do something to make it more foolproof? Sometimes, asking yourself too many "what ifs" and playing out every scenario in your head can only keep you from taking action. If the Spartans and Special Ops guys asked too many what-ifs, they would not accomplish anything. They are men of action, like how you should be as well. Moreover, focusing on the steps that you need to take promotes creativity and analytical skills.

· Be enthusiastic

Nothing is more counter-productive than someone who always drags himself to work. You should start yourself with a positive note. If you are going to attend an important meeting at work and you are one of the presenters, do not start your day by dreading what you have to do. Instead, psych yourself up.

Tell yourself that it is going to be a good day and you will slay that presentation. At first, you will feel a little silly saying positive things to yourself but this will soon become a habit if you keep doing it every day. In the movies, before soldiers go to war, you see them marching while singing something patriotic. This is their way of psyching themselves up for the major task ahead of them.

- Start with the easiest task

Before you start exercising or doing other physical activities like sports, you first need to do warm-ups. The smallest tasks will be like your warm-ups. This is also true when you take an exam. They usually advise test=takers to skip difficult questions first and just go back to them after answering all the easier ones. This is because a large task can seem overwhelming and might keep you from taking action. And once you start with the small tasks, just continue working until you finish up to the biggest tasks. As you go along, you will also gain more and more confidence. And by the time you reach the bigger and more difficult tasks, you will have enough confidence to tackle them.

- Try something different

Although it has been reiterated in this book that doing things repeatedly forms a habit and habit makes you feel more comfortable and confident in doing the task, you can also try another tactic if you find yourself stuck in rut from doing the same thing again and again. For example, if you feel yourself getting burned out from your 9 to 5 office work, you should do something that will make it a little more exciting. Quitting and changing jobs is not always an option but if you have that option, then by all means do it. If not, you can try something less drastic. Maybe you can get yourself new office clothes that will make you feel a little more excited to go to work. Or jazz up your office space a little bit. You can also befriend a coworker whom you have not gotten close to. This will make you feel a little less bored with work and will bring back a little bit of excitement when you go to work.

· Plan your future

If your future is clear to you, you will not have any reason to doubt yourself when it comes to the right paths that you need to take and the right decisions that you need to make. If you know, for instance, that you want to move to New York and you live in California, and your heart is already set, then every little thing that you will do will lead towards this future that you have already mapped out. You should also think about where you will be 10 years from now if you do not take action. If you do not save money right now, what will happen to you in the future? Picture your life in the future and what you need to do in the present will be clearer.

· Talk to a professional

If you still find yourself stuck in inactivity, and you just do not have the motivation no matter how much you try, maybe it is time to consult a professional. It might be depression or other mental health problems which require medical attention. Do not be afraid or embarrassed to seek help if you think you need it. The first step to self-improvement is acknowledging the fact that you have a problem that needs to be solved. Acknowledgment is the first step, then seeking help is the next. Once these two are done, you are on your way to becoming a more confident version of yourself.

9

Overcoming Adversities

The Special Operations Units have been through a lot more than an average person. Imagine fighting terrorists or other high-skilled opponents in unfamiliar territory, or going on a mission that is often a matter of life or death and affects not only your team but your whole country or even the whole world.

It is a tough life for them. However, you still see them overcoming one adversity after the other with confidence, as if they were born to do it. The truth is, the kind of training that these men have to go through is some of the toughest training for physical and mental toughness. An ordinary man will give up. Only the strongest and the bravest finish the training and become full-fledged Special Ops soldiers.

You can learn a lot from these tough men when it comes to overcoming adversities. Here are some of their tips.

· Prepare

In one of the previous chapters, it was mentioned that you can never fully prepare for anything. This is true but going to the war without preparing at all is another matter. You can prepare for a typhoon by stocking up on food, water, flashlights, and so on. And once the typhoon comes, you will still have to adjust and overcome minor adversities. But at least you prepared for the most part.

Over-preparing and using this as an excuse to not do something is what you should avoid. Special Ops forces are the masters of preparation. They do not go on a mission without preparing. Their whole process of preparation is intensive. After all, they will be going to a foreign place or conduct an espionage mission. These tasks require a lot of prepping and planning. They cannot just go there and rely on sheer luck because that will surely fail. When they need to go to an unfamiliar location, they would study the location as if they are Ph.D. students and the area is their research topic. They will check the topography, bodies of water, climate, weather, demography, economy, infrastructures, history, and so on. That's why they can easily blend in and working undercover is not a problem because of the kind of research they do.

You do not necessarily need to prepare as intensely and thoroughly as the Special Forces. Just make sure that your preparations are enough. You will know if it is enough when you already feel confident about what you are going to do.

· Be creative

Creativity is probably a word that is not often associated with the military. Individuality is not encouraged in the military because they have to follow orders and act as one unit. The whole idea of the military is working as one unit. If one is not cooperating, there is a big chance that the mission will fail. However, when it comes to the Special Ops soldiers, creativity is a must. This does not mean that they have painting or creative writing classes. It only means that they need to be creative when it comes to solving problems.

They should be resourceful because what they have prepared for might be completely different from the actual situation they will find themselves in. You should be able to make quick and sound decisions when the situation calls for it. When these soldiers are in the field, they do not have someone to call or ask for help if something does not go according to plan. They have to make the decisions themselves. In real life, adults often have to make major life decisions that do not only affect them but also their families. This is why you have to make your own decisions without relying on others.

Moreover, what worked for one person may not work for you. You can learn from others' experiences but you should also know how to devise your own strategy when needed. You should be adaptable and flexible. There are conventional ways of solving a certain problem but they might not be applicable in some scenarios. In this case, you have to think outside the box. The military calls this disciplined initiative. It is not a reckless risk but a calculated risk to solve a problem. You should be able to think on your own two feet and think without constraints. If you are always limited by conventions, it will be difficult to overcome adversities.

Ever heard of the story of David and Goliath? Goliath was a hulking giant but David was able to defeat him by being resourceful. He could not fight like a man normally would because he was not as big as Goliath but what he lacked in brawn he made up with his quick-thinking and resourcefulness.

- Learn how to deal with people

Most of the adversities that you face involve people. If your problems have something to do with dealing with people, then you need to know how to communicate with them. The Special Forces do not just shoot enemies. They also have to make friends with allies, or sometimes pretend to be friends with an enemy who does not know that they are working on the other side. People are probably the most difficult component of any problem because they are the most unpredictable. Special Ops soldiers are not only trained to improve their physical and mental toughness but also their interpersonal skills. These are men who work closely with soldiers from other countries who speak a different language and have a different culture. Their enemies are most likely foreigners as well. Sometimes, a successful mission does not involve shooting. It sometimes means the Special Ops men were able to strike a good deal with the enemy.

This is the same thing when it comes to overcoming adversities in real life. You need to know how to handle people. If you want to ask for a raise because your family's expenses are growing bigger, you need to know how to talk to your boss and negotiate so that you get what you want. If your wife tells you that she is thinking about getting a divorce unless you make an effort to work things out with her, then you should learn how to cooperate.

- Teach others

The best way to master something is to become a teacher. Doing something is one thing but teaching it to others is another level. Being a teacher or an expert on something can help you overcome adversities. Teaching is not just the formal way of teaching where you as a teacher are in a class with a group of people. It can also be a two-man team wherein you have to convey information before you go on your mission. More often than not, Special Operations guys work with equals or with partners rather than subordinates. This is why when they convey information, they do not give orders or commands, rather, they instruct and convey. The information and skills that you teach are based largely on the amount of knowledge that you know. The more you know, the more you can teach. This is why Special Forces make it a point to continue learning.

You can be a teacher or an expert so that you have the confidence to overcome any problem in your life. Look at life coaches and therapists. These people most likely have problems of their own but they are teachers and they know what needs to be done most of the time.

- Be motivated and take action

The motivation to overcome adversity should be there because otherwise, you will not be able to do it. You must want it badly enough if you want to overcome it. The same example as before, if your wife tells you that she wants to work things out in your marriage or she will file for a divorce, you should still want to stay married to her for you to be able to work things out. But things should not only end there. After motivation, there should be concrete action. A motivation without an action plan is just a form of cheerleading.

Motivational words like "you can do it" or "you are the best" are all meaningless if not partnered with an action plan. The plan should be concrete and viable. Your motivation for keeping your marriage intact is your love for your wife and your kids. 'Working things out' is not concrete enough. It is vague and not quantifiable. You can maybe plan to go to a marriage counselor once a week. Have open communication with your wife when things are bothering you. These concrete steps will eventually lead you to overcome this adversity in life. Your crumbling marriage is your adversity and staying happily married is the outcome.

Dealing with Bad Days

Having a bad day is normal. Everyone experienced having bad days in their lives. Even the toughest men like the Spartans and Special Ops guys. However, when things go wrong for some people, no matter how minor it is, they think it is their fault and their deficiencies that lead to these misfortunes. They then start to lose their confidence. This is what sets an ordinary man apart from the two toughest groups of men in history.

So how do you overcome bad days so that you will not lose your confidence? Here are some tips that you might want to try.

· Life is not perfect

Nothing is perfect in this world. You are just setting yourself up for disappointment if you believe that life can be perfect. It can be beautiful but not perfect. Life will always have little hiccups that you need to experience. You have your goals in life but you do not achieve these overnight, and that is normal. When you are having a bad day because you failed to achieve one goal, it's okay. Move on and learn from it. If your day was not good, you should write down your goals at the end of the day to help your mind refocus.

· Learn a lesson from every struggle

One way to look at your problems is to ask yourself the lesson that you learned from them. If you focus on everything that is going wrong with your life, you will surely feel stressed and depressed and you will lose your confidence to try. Instead, find the lesson or the major takeaway from what you are currently experiencing. Did you miss your flight? Maybe you can prevent this from happening again by asking yourself what you could have done differently to not miss your flight. Maybe you woke up late, you did not check your flight schedule, you miscalculated the time, etc. Whatever the reason is, try to improve on it next time so that this kind of thing will not happen again. If you do not learn from your bad days, then you will continue having the same problems and it will eat up your remaining self-confidence.

· It makes you appreciate your good days more

To appreciate the light, you have to experience darkness. Cheesy but true. You appreciate the positive things in your life more when you experience the negative things. Imagine dealing with a bad day successfully. You will feel like you have accomplished something spectacular and the excitement and joy are incomparable. Try to imagine the lives of people who live in less privileged countries. They do not have access to things that people who live in first-world countries take for granted like quality education, good food, clean water, and so on. It is the same thing when you are having a bad day. Your bad days make you appreciate your good days more.

· Stop worrying

If things are not going your way, worrying about them only makes you suffer twice. When you worry about the negative things in your life, for example, being late for work and its consequences, your mental health suffers. The fact that you are late and you get deducted and your boss yells at you makes you suffer a second time. If it is already out of your control, why worry about it? Just face the problem when it is already there. Otherwise, you will suffer from anxiety and panic attacks.

· Do not compare your life to others

This is one thing that you should not do when you are having a bad day. Comparing yourself to other people only makes you feel less confident about yourself and unhappy about your life. The things that you see on social media are just snippets of people's life. Do not think that their life is better than yours. Everyone has bad days, but of course, no one will be brave enough to post it on social media. The grass may look greener on the other side but that is not the case all the time. Besides, there will always be someone who is better, more beautiful, or more attractive than you and that is okay. You still need to do your own thing and not compare yourself to others because that is one surefire way to kill self-confidence.

· It is okay to ask for help

Sometimes, all you need when you are having a bad day is a shoulder to cry on or someone who will listen. Do not be ashamed to ask for help. Asking for help is a brave thing to do because you acknowledge your weakness. Some people are not comfortable doing this because they think they are exposing their vulnerable side. But if you share your problems with someone you trust, a family member or a close friend, then does it matter if they see you at your weakest? Believe it or not, people will understand because everyone has been in the same situation.

The key is that you make sure that you are sharing your woes with the right people who will be there to boost your confidence and tell you that everything is going to be okay. You have to be careful because not everyone is genuine and sincere. People with bad intentions might use the personal information that you have shared with them for their own gain or hidden agenda. You might want to turn to someone who can be sympathetic but sometimes, you also need to hear the harsh truth from someone who only wants what is best for you. Do not hesitate to ask for help. Maybe that is all you need to get through the bad days.

Remember that it is not the end of the world when things are not going your way. It happens to all people. It is not just you. Although you should not make a habit of taking comfort with the fact that other people are also suffering, that is the truth. The next day, these problems are nothing but memories and you will just laugh at them and feel silly for being too dramatic.

10

Setting Goals

You want to be self-confident in life because you have goals that you want to reach. But it also works the other way around.When you set goals, you become more confident because you know what you want in life. You should always look for the next level to keep you motivated in life. Having goals allows you to see yourself years from now. The Spartans' ultimate goal in life is to become the best warriors and to win battles. The Special Operations forces' goal is to accomplish their missions. Setting long-term goals for the future gives you a vision and short-term goals give you motivation.

You must know the proper way to set goals. You cannot simply say that you want to be successful in life because there is more to it than simply saying it. Here are the things that you need to know when it comes to goal setting.

Your Personal Goals

Most people's goal is to be successful in life. You have to be specific because your definition of success may be different from others' definition. Create a clear vision of where you see yourself in the future. This can be your personal goal.Also list the things that you have in that vision. Is it a family, your own house, a business, a higher position, etc.? Then break these down into smaller goals that you can achieve in a shorter time. Once you identify your short-term goals, you can then start working on them.

Here are the specific steps that you need to follow when it comes to setting goals.

-Set long-term goals

As discussed previously, you first need to know your long-term goals or your life goals. This does not mean that you need to plan your entire life up to your death. But ask yourself what you want to achieve in the foreseeable future. If you are not yet married, maybe you want to have your own family. Maybe you want to migrate overseas with your family. Or maybe you want to start an online business. These are major life goals that affect your decisions for you to be able to reach them.

If you are at a loss and you do not know where to begin, you can examine different areas of your life and ask yourself what you want to achieve in each of them.

- Relationship. Do you want to get married to your current partner? Are you planning to move in together? Or maybe you do not want to get married in the future?
- Family. Do you want to have kids? How many? What kind of a parent do you aim to be? Do you want to make it a point to visit your parents and siblings at least once a year?
- Career. Are you aiming for a higher position? Do you want to stay in the same company or change jobs? Are you planning to start your own business?
- Financial. What is your retirement plan? Are you planning to save up on something? What percentage of your salary are you planning to save every month?
- Physical health. Do you want to be a vegan? How much weight do you want to lose this year? Do you plan to maintain your good health until your old age?
- Mental health. Do you want to change anything in your mindset? What personality traits do you want to improve on?
- Leisure. Are there places that you want to visit? Do you want to learn a new hobby? How do you want to spend your free time?
- Altruism. Is there a charity you want to donate to? What advocacy do you want to pursue?

After categorizing different aspects of your life, you can now come up with different life goals that you want to achieve. Just do not get too excited because you might end up with so many things and you might feel overwhelmed. You should only list down the things that are close to your heart. For example, if you want to be a vegan because it is a trend right now, you should probably scrap the idea because it is not something that you want for yourself. Make sure that the goals in your list are not somebody else's goals for you. Maybe having kids is not something that you want but your parents have been bugging you about it. You have to be honest with yourself if you want to be successful in this exercise.

-Set short-term goals

These are like your supporting goals or the smaller goals that help you achieve your lifetime goals. If your life goal is achievable, say, 20 years from now, you can break down your goals into smaller ones. For example, if you want to earn a certain amount of money for retirement, you can set smaller goals every year. If you want to have your own family at the age of 35, and you are 20 right now, you can maybe write down smaller goals with their corresponding deadlines, such as get your own house, earn a specific amount every month, and so on. You can further subdivide these smaller goals into much smaller ones until they become easier for you to achieve. You divide them into smaller tasks because it makes it more realistic and it also gives you a deadline. If you do not have a deadline, it will be difficult to achieve these life goals.

Setting smaller goals also makes your progress more obvious. If the goal is too big and too far off, your progress might seem insignificant. That is why you should keep them incremental so that you know that you are achieving something.

-Stay on track

Just because you have finished writing down your goals does not mean it ends there. You have to check your goals from time to time because your circumstances might have changed over time. Maybe your salary now is bigger than when you first wrote your goals which will allow you to achieve your financial goals faster. Maybe your priorities changed because you had an unplanned pregnancy and your studies have to take a backseat. Life happens and not everything is within your control. In cases like this, you have to be open to changes and you have to be flexible.

SMART Goals

SMART is the abbreviation of the things that your goal should be like—specific, measurable, attainable, relevant, and time-bound. This makes your goal clearer ad easier to achieve. Saying that you want to travel the whole world is a vague goal. Instead, you can say 'I want to visit one country every year.

- Specific. Your goals should be specific.This means that they should be well-defined, focused, and clear. It should be detailed so that you know what you are talking about.
- Measurable. A goal that has dates, amount of money, time frames, length of time, age, and so on is measurable.
- Attainable. Your goal should also be attainable, which means that it should not be impossible to achieve.
- Relevant. For a goal to be effective, it should also be relevant or significant to your life. Do not just write a goal just because it sounds cool. It should have a significant impact on your life.
- Time-bound. Finally, a goal should be time-bound, which means that it should have a deadline.

Generic goal: I want to save money.

SMART goal: I want to save 10% of my salary every month so that I will have $XXX in 5 years.

Generic goal: I want to have kids.

SMART goal: I want to have 2 kids by the time I reach 40.

Generic goal: I want to buy a house.

SMART goal: I want to buy a small townhouse near the city which costs not more than $xxxx by the end of the year.

Goal-setting Tips

- State a positive goal statement. If you want to become a manager in your current company, do not say something along the lines of 'do not remain in the same position'. Phrase it in such a way that it brings positivity and motivation to your life rather than negativity and bitterness.
- You might have a lot of goals but you have to make sure that you prioritize the things that matter most in your life and the ones that require urgent attention. For instance, if you want to be a vegan but you are also trying to gain a little bit of weight because of an eating disorder, maybe you should focus on your health first before you decide to become a vegan. Or if you want to save money for buying a car but you need money for medication, you should use the money for your medication because the car can wait but your health cannot.
- You need to allocate resources to achieve your goals. All goals need time, money, or/and effort. This is something that you should be willing to spend if you want to achieve your goals. Whether it needs money, time, or effort, you should have all three at your disposal for you to move forward in achieving your goal. Some goals might require the help of other people. If this is the case, you need to speak to that person so that both of you are on the same page. This is often seen in families or couples who usually share the same goals. Conflicts arise if both their resources are required but they do not see eye to eye.

- Once a goal is achieved, whether it is a small goal or a big goal, you need to celebrate it. You can reward yourself for accomplishing a small goal by simply taking a day off from work, eating out with your partner, and so on. If a major goal is achieved, you can celebrate it by buying something for yourself, going out of town, and so on. The reward should match the goal that you just accomplished. If it is a small goal and you celebrated big time, then it is like wasting resources. And how would you celebrate bigger goals then? If it is a major goal and you just gave yourself a small pat on the back, you might feel a little unappreciated after all the hard work you have put into it. You have to know how to properly celebrate and reward yourself depending on the type of goal you accomplished.
- If the goal is too easy to achieve, maybe you can try to make it a little harder next time. Tell yourself, since I can easily do this, maybe I can push myself a little further next time so that I can accomplish my goal faster. For example, if your goal is to finish cleaning one room in one day, but you were able to finish one room in just over an hour, then maybe you can proceed to the next room. This way, you will finish your goal within a shorter time. Just do not push yourself too much or you will end up feeling burned out.

11

Good Habits and Bad Habits

Self-discipline is needed to break bad habits and create good ones. Once you start breaking your bad habits and forming good habits, you will feel better about yourself and you will start having the confidence that you need. It makes you feel confident about yourself because you know that you are in control of your life. Habits are a big part of who you are as a person. But you have to remember that you are the one who makes them. It is in your power to either break free or start a new one.

How can you tell if your habit is bad? Some of them are pretty obvious, like smoking, being late, and so on. Others are not so obvious. One way to tell if it is a bad habit is when it interrupts your life. For instance, browsing online before you go to bed for several hours without noticing it is a bad habit because you do not get the right amount of sleep. Checking your phone while having dinner with your family is also a bad habit because it stops you from having a meaningful conversation with them. The negative effects are not so obvious but they surely affect your life in a negative way. Bad habits can ruin your physical or mental health, relationships, career, and other aspects of your life. They are also a waste of time, energy, and money.

You might ask now, then why not just stop? Why keep doing these bad habits if you know that they only make your life miserable? Maybe you think it is as simple as that but like most things in this life, it is easier said than done. You probably know at least one person who has a bad habit. Maybe you have a bad habit that you are not aware of. Do you think it is easy for a smoker to simply quit smoking? Some can do it cold turkey, while others have to take little steps or they will suffer from withdrawal symptoms.

To solve any problem in life, you first need to identify the root causes.

Two Major Causes of Bad Habits

Stress and boredom are the two main culprits why people form bad habits. When you are bored or stressed, you will do something to alleviate that feeling. And before you know it, every time you feel bored or stressed, you will automatically do it without thinking. It could be biting your nails, binge eating, binge-watching, and overspending, non-stop online browsing, and so on.

There are two ways that a bad habit disrupts your life. First, you waste your time, energy, and money by doing these habits. You shop for things you do not need to cope with stress. You watch an entire series in one sitting because you feel bored. These are resources—money and time—that can be used doing something more productive. Another way that it affects you is that it becomes a tool for procrastination.

The good news is that instead of dealing with stress and boredom in a negative and destructive way, why not teach yourself positive ways to cope. You can form good habits that will serve as a substitute for these bad habits. But before you do this, ask yourself if there is a deeper cause to your boredom and stress. Again, you have to still dig deeper and identify the root cause so that it can be addressed properly. Maybe the stress and boredom that you feel are just the tips of the iceberg. Maybe there is something more to it than meets the eye, something deeper and more serious. It can be fear, a past event that had a major negative impact on your life, a limiting view about yourself, etc. Be honest about yourself and seek professional help if necessary. You must understand the causes of these bad habits so that it will be easier to turn them into positive habits.

Replacing Bad Habits with Good Ones

Your habits, whether good or bad, are part of who you are. And if that is the case, do you want to be defined with negative habits or positive ones? Moreover, habits provide some form of benefits one way or another, whether the habit is good or bad. For instance, smoking does calm your nerves and makes you think clearly but everyone knows that it is bad for your health. Bad habits such as gnawing on your nails, clenching your jaw, or tapping your foot are also beneficial because they help relieve stress but you know they are not good for your body and in a social setting.

When you come to the office, the first thing you do before you go about your day is check your emails. This makes you feel connected and that you are not missing out on anything important, but at the same time it makes you distracted because it divides your attention between the tasks that you have to do right away and the new tasks that you have just seen in your emails.

This only shows that bad habits are difficult to break, no matter how small, because they give you something in return—a positive feeling that you need at that particular moment. People who gamble or use drugs are after the high that they feel when they win or while they are under the influence. What you need to do instead of telling yourself to stop is to replace this bad habit with a good one that will give you the same feeling.

Instead of telling yourself to stop smoking, you can instead find a healthier alternative to cope with stress. Maybe you can do short exercises that will help you deal with stress.

Breaking Your Bad Habits

There are some ways that you can try to break your bad habits. Here are ideas that you might want to try.

· Find a healthier alternative

You need to come up with a substitute that will not have any negative impact on your life but will give you the same feeling as your bad habit. If you tend to binge eat when you are bored or under a lot of stress, maybe you can try another activity such as gardening, crocheting, sewing, and so on. Learning a new hobby can help you break from your bad habit. You should know what to do when you think you are about to do that same bad habit. When you feel boredom kicking in and you have the urge to browse Facebook, which you know will lead you to waste several hours of your life, you need to have a plan ready. Maybe you can instead grab a vacuum and start cleaning.

· Remove things that trigger your bad habits

You know yourself well so you would know the things that trigger your bad habits. If you browse social media before going to bed, then turn off your phone or your wifi so that you cannot go online. If you tend to smoke after drinking alcohol, then do not drink alcohol. If you cannot stop watching a whole series until you finish each episode, then do not start watching. Avoiding the triggers that cause your bad habits is a great way to break free from them.

Make sure you change your environment and the things around you to help you break your bad habits and form new good ones.

· Do it with somebody

Some people do not want to tell others about their goals of breaking their bad habits because they do not want others to see them fail. But that is the point. You should tell others so that you have more motivation not to fail. How many times have you started a new diet without telling anyone? Every New Year, you probably have a long list of resolutions that remained as that—just long lists of resolutions. This is because you are not being held accountable. You are not as committed to your goal because it is just you and no one will know if you fail. You can just stop doing it anytime if you think you cannot do it. But if you are serious about breaking your bad habit, then you should find someone that you can pair up with who will check on your progress. It is even much better if this person has the same goal so that you can do things together. You can also celebrate your victories together. It is nice to have someone to be with and who understands when you are in the process of changing for the better.

In line with this, you need to surround yourself with people who will help you achieve your goals. If you are trying to stop eating too many sweets but your partner keeps devouring cakes and cookies in front of you, then it will be difficult for you to quit. It is also disrespectful to do that to someone who is trying to break from bad habits. If you are a drug user and you want to change, but your friends are also drug users, then you will not be able to stop doing it. Make sure that the people around you support your endeavors and want to help you change for the better.

· You are not trying to be someone else

Your habits are indeed a part of who you are, but you can easily change them. It is up to you because it is your life. That does not mean that you are trying to be someone else. It only means that you are trying to improve yourself and to become a better person. You do not need a personality overhaul just to break from your bad habit. It does not mean that you are changing to a different person. The truth is that these habits have just developed as you started living your life. They were not there from the beginning which means that at some point in your life, you were free from these habits. If you look at it this way, it only means that you are just trying to go back to your old self and not trying to be someone you are not. You are not trying to be a non-smoker, you are returning to being a non-smoker. It may have been a long time ago but it was still you and if you were able to do it before, there is no reason why you cannot do it now.

· Prepare rebuttals for your negative thoughts

Some people find it difficult to break from their bad habits because they think that they are weak human beings. This is true to a certain degree but this does not mean that you have to sink in despair and just let yourself be eaten up by your negative thoughts and habits. Every time you find yourself giving up, thinking that it is just who you are as a person and you cannot change, you need to come up with a rebuttal. For example, if you find yourself thinking that you are a failure because something so simple as losing weight is difficult for you, you can say something like 'but I am trying now to become healthier'.

· There will be failures

You are human, you are not perfect. It is not an excuse; it is just what it is. You will find yourself failing once or twice on your journey to a better you. You might even give in to temptation one day and eat a bag of potato chips when you are trying to stay away from junk food. You might skip a day of workout because you feel tired. It is okay. Cut yourself some slack. The key thing to remember is that there are a lot more victories than failures. This does not mean that you can now go easy on yourself because it is okay to make mistakes. That's not how it works. You need to learn from these mistakes. Maybe next time, you should plan for these kinds of scenarios so that you will not get off track. What matters most is that you bounce back and you do not fall into a downward spiral just because of one small screw-up.

12

Live a Life Free from Fear to Achieve Self-Love

The main point of this book is to live life with self-confidence by eliminating fear, like how the Spartans and Special Operations forces live their life. Fear is a big deterrent and should be eliminated so that you can live with confidence and self-love. Here are some things that you should keep in mind to live a life free from fear and to learn to love yourself.

· Let go of preconceived notions

If you want to pursue a degree but are scared because you are already in your

40s, just stop worrying and go for it. Studying is not only for young people. There are already a lot of success stories about older adults who decided to go back to the university to pursue a degree. It is never too late to do anything you want.

It's similar to fashion. Some colors are associated with different seasons. Bright colors for summer, pastel for spring, warm tones for fall, and neutrals for winter. Who says you cannot wear pastel in the fall season while eating hot cross buns? Sometimes, these preconceived notions keep us from doing things. And the funny thing is, they sometimes do not make sense at all. So ask yourself, why am I doing or not doing this? Is it because society expects or does not expect me to do this? Think outside the box and re-evaluate your life.

- Focus on what you can do

Instead of focusing on the things that you cannot do, why not focus on the things that you can? If you are afraid to speak in public because you feel like you are not that articulate when speaking, why focus on that? Instead, focus on your sincerity and genuine interest in the subject matter. If you are interested in what you are going to talk about, you will learn how articulate you can be. By focusing on the things that you can do, you discover new talents that you do not know you have. Who would have thought that you can speak that well in public when you are talking about your advocacy? Turns out you only need to find the right topic to be able to speak well in front of a lot of people.

- Learn more about the things that scare you

Fear comes from not knowing something. The fear of the unknown is real. The space is scary because man can only study a small part of it. It is the same thing with what's at the bottom of the ocean. It is scary because you do not know anything about it. If you are afraid of something, maybe you just need to learn more about the thing that scares you. For example, if you are afraid of flying, maybe you should do some research about the science behind airplanes and how they work. This way, you know that science is keeping it from crashing. You should also tell yourself that there are already so many people who have successfully traveled by air. Thousands of people travel by airplane every day. There are accidents but it is just like any other form of transportation. Once you learn more about it, you might feel less scared next time you fly. Who knows, you might even enjoy air travel.

· Pick your battles

The things that you experience in life do not have equal importance. You need to know which ones you will tackle and which ones you will just let go of. If you are afraid of spiders but you do not come across a lot of spiders in your life, then you can just let it go. But if you are an ecologist who has to visit forests or shrubbery, then you might want to overcome this fear. Choose the ones that you need to overcome because it keeps you from functioning well in society. Maybe when you have the time, you can tackle your fear of spiders but for now, just let it go.

· Be with the right people

You may not notice it but the people around you play a big role in how you handle problems in life. If you are in a relationship with a toxic person, chances are he will not be able to help you overcome your fears. He might even be contributing to your anxiety. But if you are with positive people who believe in yourself and whom you can trust, then overcoming your fears will be easy.

You will still come across people who are toxic and manipulative no matter how much you try to avoid them. They may be a coworker or a person in your group of friends. If you are not comfortable with someone, try not to be in the same room with that person as much as you can. If he says something insulting, tell him cordially that you will not allow yourself to be disrespected. You can either report this to HR or your boss. If he is a friend, try to cut ties and just be with the ones who matter. Pretty soon they will catch up and learn why you decide to cut that person from your life and do the same thing themselves.

- Tell yourself you are a survivor

Everyone who is still living and breathing is a survivor, including you. You have most likely faced a lot of problems in life but you are still here. You have been through a lot but you never gave up. So why stop now? You are a survivor who has made it through the most difficult times in your life. It's just public speaking, you can do it. You were able to give birth or support your family during the recession, so do not be scared about something as trivial as public speaking. You have made it this far. You did it and you will do it again. You just need to believe in yourself and trust that you can do it. Tell yourself that in the grand scheme of things, the things that you are scared of are just specks. So do not lose faith in yourself.

Conclusion

Thank you for downloading the book! Now that you know about the mindsets of tough individuals like the Spartans and Special Operations units, you can now apply what you have learned in this book.

Having self-confidence and loving yourself is not as easy as it sounds, especially to people who have been struggling with having confidence since they were young. There are so many things that you can do to improve your self-confidence.

The most important takeaways from this book is to make sure that you constantly improve yourself as a person and you change your mindset by following the hundreds of tips that you can find in each chapter. Thankfully, books like this exist. Hope you learn a lot and start living a life free from fear and worries.

Thank You

Finally, if you enjoyed this book, then I'd like to ask you for a favor. Would you be kind enough to leave a review for this book ? It'd be greatly appreciated!

Thank you and good luck!

Copyright

of the trademark is without permission or backing by the trademark owner. All trademarks and brands within this book are for clarifying purposes only and are the owned by the owners themselves, not affiliated with this document.

.

Made in the USA
Monee, IL
25 November 2021

83006290R00069